THE
EUROPEAN
OVERLAND ROUTES

THE EUROPEAN OVERLAND ROUTES

Adapted from TO THE ENDS OF THE EARTH
Irene M. Franck and David M. Brownstone

A Volume in the Trade and Travel Routes Series

Facts On File

New York • Oxford • Sydney

The European Overland Routes

Facts on File, Inc.
460 Park Avenue South
New York NY 10016
USA

Facts On File Limited
Collins Street
Oxford OX4 1XJ
United Kingdom

Facts On File Ltd Pty
Talavera & Khartoum Rds
North Ryde NSW 2113
Australia

Library of Congress Cataloging-in-Publication Data

The European overland routes: adapted from To the ends of the earth
   by Irene M. Franck and David M. Brownstone.
      p.   cm. — (Trade and travel routes series)
   Bibliography: p.
   Includes index.
      Summary: A historical survey of the Amber Routes, the Appian Way,
   the Egratian Way, the Great North Road, the Heraclean Way, and the
   Orient Route.
      ISBN 0-8160-1877-4
      1. Trade routes—Europe—History—Juvenile literature. [1. Trade
   routes—Europe—History.] I. Franck, Irene M. To the ends of the
   earth. II. Series.
   HE361.E87 1990
   382'.094—dc20   89-11694

British and Australian CIP data available on request from Facts On File.

Facts On File books are available at special discounts when purchased in bulk quantities for businesses, associations, institutions or sales promotion. Please contact the Special Sales Department of our New York office at 212/683-2244 (dial 800/322-8755 except in NY, AK, or HI).

Jacket design by Catherine Hyman
Composition by Facts On File, Inc.
Manufactured by R.R. Donnelley & Sons
Printed in the United States of America

10 9 8 7 6 5 4 3 2 1

This book is printed on acid-free paper.

CONTENTS

LIST OF MAPS

PREFACE

The European Overland Routes is one volume in the Trade and Travel Routes series. The series itself is based on our earlier work, *To The Ends of the Earth*, published by Facts On File, Inc., in 1984. This adaptation of the work for young readers has been prepared by Facts On File; many new illustrations have also been added.

Several publishers gave permission to reprint selections from their works. In this volume, excerpts on pp. 48-49 are from Horace's *Satires, Epistles and Ars Poetica*, translated by Harvard University in the Loeb Classical Library in 1926, copyright © Harvard University Press. The maps, drawn from the original work, are by Dale Adams.

Irene M. Franck
David M. Brownstone

INTRODUCTION

WHAT IS A TRADE ROUTE?

In a world without airplanes, engine-powered ships, trucks, or even paved roads, how did people journey from one place to another? How did products that were found only in a very small part of the world eventually find their way across the continents? For almost five thousand years, people have been bringing products from one part of the world to another using trade routes. Traders from Europe, Asia, and Africa carried furs, spices, silks, pottery, knives, stone utensils, jewels, and a host of other commodities, exchanging the products found in one area for the products found in another.

When trading first began, there were no real roads. Local traders might follow trails or cross steep mountain passes in their treks from one village to another. With the passage of time, tracks might be widened and eventually paved. But the new paved roads tended to follow the old trade routes, establishing these routes as important links of communication between different cultures.

As technology advanced, sea-lanes became vital trade routes between the various continents, and made possible trade with North America, South America, and Australia. Many of the highways and seaways that have been used predominantly for trade throughout history have shaped its course of events because of the many ways in which the routes have been used.

WHY STUDY TRADE ROUTES?

Studying the trade routes is one way of learning about the history of the world. As we look at the trade routes of Europe, for example, we see how the nations of that continent have changed throughout the centuries: We learn how Scandinavian Vikings came to sail south and west to settle in France and Britain; we can appreciate how present-day Hungary was originally settled by a wandering tribe from the Ural Mountains, etc. In a similar way, by looking at the trade routes of Africa, we can trace the history of the slave trade and learn about the European colonization of Africa in the 18th and 19th centuries.

In addition, studying the trade routes helps us better understand the origin of many of the institutions and services with which we are familiar today. Postal systems, tolls, guidebooks, roadside restaurants and hotels all came into being, either directly or indirectly, because of trade routes. Studying the trade routes will help you to understand how they emerged.

How to Use This Book

This book is organized in chapters. Each chapter is devoted to the history of one trade route, or in some cases, where the particular trade route has an especially long and eventful past, to a particular era in a trade route's history. Therefore, you can simply read about one trade route that particularly interests you or, alternatively, read about all the trade routes in a given area. At the end of each chapter, you will find a list of books for further reading, which will assist you in locating additional sourcebooks should you need them to support report research or classroom work. If you are using these books as references for a particular history course, check the index of each to find the subject or person you need to know more about. The list of maps at the front of this book will direct you to all maps contained herein, and thereby help you to locate each trade route on the face of the earth.

Studying trade routes can be a fascinating way of learning about world history—and of understanding more about our lives today. We hope you enjoy all the volumes in the Trade and Travel Routes series.

1

THE AMBER ROUTES

AMBER: THE ELECTRIC JEWEL

Amber is a gold-colored stone-like material that is often used in jewelry. Although it looks like a jewel, amber is actually a hardened lump of resin from an evergreen tree, like a pine or fir. When you rub amber with a piece of cloth, it gives off static electricity. In fact, the word *electricity* is derived from *elektron*, the Greek word for amber.

Amber has been valued by people for thousands of years. In most cases, men and women have used this precious substance in jewelry and ornaments. However, on the southern coast of the Baltic Sea—land that today constitutes northern Poland and Germany—the waves used to wash lots of amber up onto the sandy beaches. Amber was so plentiful here that the Greek explorer Pytheas actually found people burning it for fuel.

Amber had another unusual use in Rome in the days of the Roman Empire. When Nero was emperor, he used to hold circuses in which men called *gladiators* would fight with wild beasts in a big arena. Before the beasts were ready to fight, they would be held back with big nets. One Roman knight once brought back so much amber it was used to decorate the beasts' nets! Amber was also used to decorate the gladiators' swords, shields, and other equipment. Most amber is found in small pieces, smaller than a golf ball—but this knight brought back a piece of amber so big that it weighed 13 pounds.

Some of the first trading routes to reach across Europe to Asia were beaten through forests and over mountains by people carrying amber from one village to the next. People traded it for stone knives and axes, for salt, for furs and for many other things they wanted

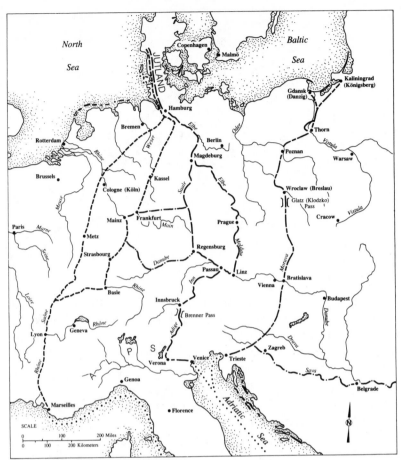

The Amber Routes in Prehistoric Times
(Modern Cities Noted for Reference)

— — — Brenner Pass Route
- - - - - - - Rhône-Saône Route
— · — · — Vistula Route

— · · — · · — Main Connecting Land Routes
· · · · · · · · Main Connecting Sea Routes

or needed. These trade routes started more than 4,000 years ago, and they covered a surprising amount of distance.

THE ARCHAEOLOGIST DETECTIVES

We know about the origins of the amber trading routes because of what *archaeologists* have found out. Archaeologists study the life and culture of people of the past through looking at artifacts and buildings these people have left behind. For example, archaeologists might dig in the area where an ancient city once stood. They might find the remains of old buildings, and would then have to figure out

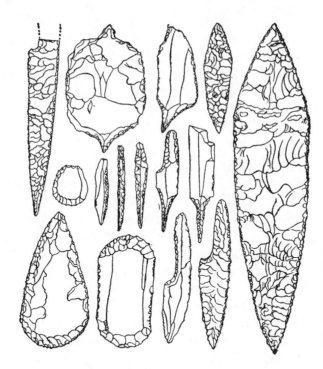

The early Amber Routes were opened by traveling peddlers who made, repaired, and sold flint tools and weapons like these. (From James Henry Breasted, *Ancient Times: A History of the Early World*, 1914)

what the buildings had originally looked like and what they were used for. Or they might find a broken piece of an old pot, and would use it to figure out what these ancient people had eaten and how they had lived.

Archaeologists have been able to find out about the amber routes because amber lasts a long time. Amber is really a kind of *fossil*, which means that the organic resin that forms it has gone through a chemical process that makes it hard and stonelike. Therefore, archaeologists have been able to find amber in places where it was left several thousand years ago.

In the early days of trading, traders traveled only on foot and had to carry everything they sold. So the early peddlers carried only some of their precious goods, leaving the rest in hiding places along the route. Travel was very dangerous in those days. Traders might be ambushed by robbers, killed by wild beasts, or simply become lost in the woods on a poorly marked trail. Many traders never lived to come back for the goods they had hidden so carefully. Thousands of years later, archaeologists have found the secret hoards and road-side graves, and have used them to trace the long-ago trading routes.

Other goods besides the amber have survived the thousands of years between then and now. Archaeologists have found stone knives and axes, perhaps prepared by the traders themselves.

Imagine how important such products must have been to the early farmers living in isolated villages. We also know that traders carried salt, fur, ivory (from Africa and Asia), and cowrie shells (from the Indian Ocean or Southern Pacific Ocean).

THE THREE MAIN AMBER ROUTES

The Brenner Pass Route. This is the oldest of the three amber routes. We don't even know how old it is, but the archaeologists guess that it is over 4,000 years old. It seems to have begun in present-day Denmark, passed through the countries that are now Germany, Czechoslovakia, and Austria, crossed the high mountain range of the Alps and ended in modern-day Italy.

Of course, when this route first began, these countries did not exist in their present-day form. People lived in villages and towns all over the continent of Europe, but they did not have the sense of themselves as citizens of a nation. Imagine how isolated they were. They only had a sense of themselves as members of the village and the tribe or family that they knew. Perhaps they were also aware of neighboring villages a day or two's journey away. Of course, they knew that the traders came from foreign lands—but what they

From the region of modern Verona, in Italy, the old Amber Route leads north through the Alps by way of the gentle Brenner Pass. (By A. H. Hallam Murray, *Sketches on the Old Road Through France to Florence*, 1904)

called "foreign lands" might have been as close as what for us today would be a car ride of half a day!

The isolation was so great that people spoke many different languages, many different variations of what would eventually become the languages French, German, Italian, etc. Because people lived so far apart, it might be that two people speaking the same language would have such different *dialects* that they would not be able to understand each other. (Dialects emerge within the same language, usually as a result of people going to live in different areas, and differ in certain words and pronunciation.) In this world of scattered towns and villages, traders were very important. Besides carrying goods, they carried information, a sense of what was happening in the rest of the world.

Traders along the Brenner Pass Route faced an especially difficult obstacle—the Alps. The peaks of the sprawling mountain range are so high that they are always covered with snow, no matter what the season. Yet the early traders discovered a pass—a way through the mountains—the 4,500-foot-high Brenner Pass. (As you can guess, that's the pass the route was named for.)

Over the centuries, the wandering merchants gradually improved the Brenner Pass Route. They found new *fords*—places where streams and rivers were shallow enough to cross on foot. Good fords were necessary, because even if traders did know how to swim, it wouldn't have been very practical to swim across a river while carrying a load of stone axes! Sometimes traders would build simple wooden bridges. To get through a marsh, they might make a "corduroy road"—layers of logs laid one on top of the other. Of course, these improvements happened very slowly. Imagine what would happen if one trader made a corduroy and then no other trader passed that way for a whole year. Think of what the rain and snow would do to wooden logs lying in a marsh through the winter and spring.

The Rhône-Saône Route. The second amber route began like the first and passed from present-day Denmark into what is now Germany. The route then branched off in two directions, south and west along the Rhine and Saône Rivers (through today's Germany and Switzerland), then more sharply southwest along the Saône and Rhône Rivers down through today's France to the Mediterranean Sea. This route was opened after about 1800 B.C., during the *Bronze Age*.

The Bronze Age is the archaeologists' name for that time in history when human beings first learned how to work with metal. The first metal that people worked with was bronze, which is an *alloy*, or mixture, of copper, tin, phosphorus, zinc, and sometimes some other elements as well. Bronze is hard enough to be used for tools and weapons. Learning how to mix or *cast* bronze was a great discovery because of all the new things that could be made.

Before the Bronze Age had been the *Stone Age*. As the name suggests, during that time people knew how to make things only out of stone. Axes, knives, utensils, tools for digging—all had to be carved out of stone. When people discovered how to use bronze, they could make these things out of metal, instead.

During the Bronze Age traders began to carry bronze artifacts instead of stone artifacts. Like the traders of the Stone Age, a Bronze Age trader might offer to repair an item that had been broken. Or he might trade a new item for an old, broken one, fix the old item and then sell it as new at the next stop on his route. Thousands of years later, archaeologists would be able to tell how old a route was by whether they found bronze or stone items in the hiding places along the route.

Archaeologists could tell that the Rhône-Saône Route had been dangerous because they found the remains of wrecked ferries that never made it across the Rhine River. They have also found robbers' storage sites along the routes—for, like the traders, robbers could not always carry everything they "owned."

The eastern branch of the Rhône-Saône Route had a special advantage: the local, Alpine peoples worked the amber into ornaments before it was sent on. These ancestors of the modern-day Swiss had a wide reputation as good artisans. The Etruscan people, who lived in northwest Italy, sent their amber north to be worked on by these fine jewelry- and ornament-makers.

Amber was used to decorate all kinds of things; thousands of years ago amber filled the holes in this ivory-carved Spartan warship. (Museum, Sparta)

The Vistula Route. The third and youngest of the amber routes is the Vistula Route. It began in the coastlands of the Eastern Baltic Sea, which were so rich in amber that people burned these "jewels" for fuel. Even before 2000 B.C., there had been an amber route from this area to Central Europe and Russia, but that trade was later cut off. In about 1000 B.C., a new route was opened.

This route began in present-day Poland, continued through central Europe and today's Yugoslavia, and finished at the Mediterranean Sea. By the time this route was opened, the amber trade was more highly organized. That meant that many parts of the route were improved, because more people were using it and could help keep it up. Some of the marshes and muddy roads that were "corduroyed"—covered with wooden logs—were preserved in good condition until modern times.

Archaeologists have also found exposed bedrock along the route, with old grooves cut into the rock. From these old markings they

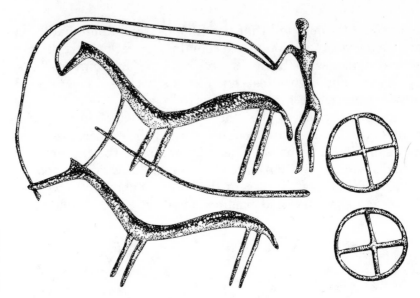

Chariots like this one from Sweden were used throughout Europe by about 1500 B.C. (Historiska Museum, Stockholm)

have established that the carts that traveled along this route were about one yard wide, from wheel to wheel. Once traders began using carts, they could carry many more goods. Archaeologists have found some trader storage sites holding over a ton of amber—some of it rough cut, some partly worked into ornaments. The old traders may have done some of their work at these sites, because archaeologists have also found a wide range of tools.

The Etruscans and the Greeks

Two of the earliest great European civilizations were those of the Etruscans and of the Greeks. These two civilizations took part in the trade of amber, which they used for ornaments and jewelry.

The Etruscans. This people lived in *Etruria*, a region of present-day Italy. They migrated there from Asia Minor (the area around present-day Turkey) in about 1200 B.C., and evolved a distinctive culture that reached its peak of power and wealth around 600 B.C. Their civilization began to decline through the fifth and fourth centuries B.C., when another group of people in Italy, the Romans, began to take power. Until that time, however, they were major consumers of amber, especially of the fine ornaments of the Alpine craftspeople that were brought via the Rhône-Saône Route. The Etruscans often traded for amber with a new group of traders who were exploring that route—the Greeks.

The Greeks. The Greek civilization flourished in what is today the country of Greece. The ancient Greeks developed ideas of philosophy, politics, and art that are still very influential in Western Europe and the United States today. They were the first people to live by democratic principles: the citizens themselves decided how the country was to be governed. A Greek scientist and philosopher, Lucretius, came up with the first theory of the atom. Greek art, which tried to use a knowledge of anatomy to make figures seem "real," influenced Western European art for thousands of years.

What we call "Ancient Greece" was actually several different cultures, as different peoples fanned out into the archipelago of peninsulas and islands and established their own Greek dialect and their own way of life. The Golden Age of Ancient Greece is considered to start at about 500 B.C., the beginning of a period that saw many discoveries in art and philosophy that are still influential today.

By 146 B.C., the Golden Age of Greece was over and Greece was under the control of a new master, the Roman Republic, which was based in what is today the country of Italy. The Romans had always been very much influenced by the Greeks in art and politics—and in fashion as well. In 400 B.C., amber had been out of fashion in Greece for a while. At about this same time, when the Romans were beginning to extend their power in Italy, they too, following the lead of the Greeks, became less interested in amber. The amber market dropped sharply. Trade continued along the amber routes—after all, people still wanted to buy bronze items, salt, and furs—but it had been the desire for amber that really kept business going before. By the time amber came back into fashion, the European world had become quite a different place. The Roman Empire now controlled big portions of Europe, including much of the territory that the amber routes passed through. The Romans changed the parts of the amber routes they controlled from rough trails into paved, protected Roman roads.

THE ROADS OF THE ROMAN EMPIRE

The Roman Empire began as the tiny city of Rome, located on seven hills. This modest city grew to be an empire that extended through much of modern Europe and Asia, controlling vast territories by means of its huge armies. The Romans enslaved people from the areas they conquered, and imposed heavy taxes and other burdens on these peoples. They also helped overcome the isolation of these areas, connecting them to one another as common parts of the

Roman Empire. One of the main ways that the Romans connected their empire was by means of roads.

The Early Romans. The early Romans were farmers who lived around the seven hills on the Tiber River. They paid little attention to the amber routes, happy only to receive the traders that brought them goods from far away. The city of Rome was once ruled by the Etruscans, until about 500 B.C., when Romans overthrew these "outsiders" and established a Roman Republic.

As we have seen, the Romans came into contact with the Greeks, which greatly affected their culture. They also extended their rule over what had been Etruria. By the third century B.C., the Romans controlled central and southern Italy.

Beginnings of Empire. In the first century B.C., Julius Caesar invaded Gaul, the area that is modern France. He pushed a new road through the Alps, following an earlier trader's path along the 8,000-foot-high Great St. Bernard Pass. By 50 B.C., he had conquered Gaul for Rome and further extended the route through the Alps.

Caesar was assassinated in 44 B.C., as described in Shakespeare's play, *Julius Caesar*. Rome was then ruled by a *triumvirate*, or group of three men. Two of these three men are still well-known: Caesar's grandnephew Octavian and Marc Antony. This group dissolved in fighting, with Octavian opposing Antony and Antony's ally Cleopatra, the queen of Egypt. You can read Shakespeare's version of these events in the play *Antony and Cleopatra*.

The victor in these battles was Octavian, who took the name *Augustus* and became the first Roman emperor. He was the one who organized the Roman army into the force that conquered so much of the rest of the world, ensuring a period of some 200 years that marked the height of the Roman Empire.

Building the Roads. In order to have access to its vast territories, Rome needed roads. Roman governors needed roads in order to ride into the lands that the emperor sent them to rule. They needed roads to receive messages from the emperor and to send messages back to him. Roads could be used by traders buying goods in one part of the vast empire and selling them in another. But, most important to the ancient Romans, roads were needed for armies to march on. Armies needed firm, wide roads that could be used in all weather by soldiers traveling from Rome into the lands that Rome ruled.

The Romans were good engineers. They built roads to fit the kind of country they passed through; the most distinctive feature of Roman roads is that the are always straight. In mountainous or rocky country, Roman engineers had their workers carve roads out of the sides of hills. They built drainage ditches by the roads, so that water could run off in rainy weather. They paved the roads with stone, so that mud would not make travel impossible.

But in the lowlands of northern Gaul the Romans used the road-building methods that had already been used in the region for over 2,000 years. They built log roads 10 feet wide over marshy regions. Sometimes they added a top layer of gravel or sand, for firmer footing. In southern Gaul, the Romans built heavy stone bridges. But in the lowlands, wooden bridges were more common. Sometimes these were movable *pontoon* bridges. A pontoon bridge is something like a string of wooden barrels all tied to each other, each floating in the water. These bridges were movable, but they could also be covered with earth and gravel when they were in one place.

The Romans counted on their log roads and bridges when they wanted to invade Germania (present-day Germany). They used the old amber routes as part of their invasion plan, and built log roads

Once they had built their fine roads and bridges, Romans could travel around in horse-drawn carts like this one. (Landesmuseum, Trèves)

into the country for their soldiers to march on. But the Romans were defeated and had to stop at the Rhine River. From that time onwards they used the Rhine as a frontier, which they fortified against people who might want to invade *them*.

Everywhere that the Romans built roads, trade flourished. Traders could count on roads that would be passable in all weather, even by horse-drawn or ox-drawn carts. The Romans built roads through the Alps as well as along the old amber routes. Some of the roads—used mainly by soldiers—ran along sheer cliffsides overlooking deep mountain canyons. These hard routes have become modern highways, but because they were so difficult to use, they never replaced the old amber routes for the Romans.

Travelers and Traders. All sorts of people used the Roman roads once the new construction made travel easier and safer. The main roads, of course, were the smoothest and safest of all. One Roman emperor, Claudius, had a special carriage built so that he could play dice as he rode through Gaul. The side routes were not as good. The Roman writer Apuleius wrote that they were rough tracks "heavily rutted, now a morass of stagnant water, now covered by a layer of slippery mud."

In some parts of Gaul, the roads were over 25 feet wide. Farmers could use these roads to drive herds of cattle to nearby cities, even to Rome itself, in search of the best market prices.

The soldiers that used these roads made their camps each night along the side of the road. Other travelers had to find their own places to stay. If possible, a traveler stayed with friends, for that way a safe and comfortable place was certain.

Everyone else had to make do with inns, the ancestors of our modern-day hotels and motels. The old inns were dangerous places. A traveling stranger might even be kidnapped into slavery at one of them. Even when they were safe, these inns were not very comfortable. Apuleius complained, "My couch [that is, the bed where he slept], besides being rather short, had a leg missing and was worm-eaten!"

When people were traveling along a route for long periods of time, road travel could be rather boring. Therefore, those traveling together for safety's sake got into the habit of telling each other stories to pass the time. This practice lasted well into medieval times. A great work of literature, Chaucer's *Canterbury Tales*, is about a group of travelers telling each other sad, funny, and romantic stories. In the days before radio and television, people made their own entertainment.

Travelers were in a peculiar bind. Because they didn't want to be attacked by robbers, they often banded together in large groups. But sometimes such large groups were suspected as robbers themselves. Apuleius tells one frightening story:

> When the farmers on a country estate near which we were passing saw us in such numbers, they thought we were brigands ... They sent after us huge dogs. [Some of the dogs were] enormous, savage creatures, accustomed to feeding on corpses left in the fields and trained in addition to bite ... all passing wayfarers.

THE DECLINE OF ROME

Although the Romans sent troops and Roman governors to rule the conquered lands, they also traded with their subject peoples, and allowed them to settle in Rome and do business there. There were revolts and uprisings—most notably the revolt led by Spartacus, a slave who helped organize other slaves into an army that fought for its freedom. Ultimately, however, the revolt of Spartacus was put down and, for the most part, the conquered peoples accepted Roman rule.

However, by the third century A.D., peoples from the East were pushing into the Roman Empire. Many of these were nomadic people who would not settle on Roman lands and accept Roman rule. The Huns, Vandals, Goths, and other peoples made their way westward from the plains of central Asia (present-day Russia, Mongolia, and other eastern countries). Three of these peoples—The Burgundians, the Franks, and the Lombards—gave their names to the areas where they eventually settled: *Burgundy* in modern-day *France* and *Lombardy* in modern-day Italy. The Huns eventually settled in *Hungary*, driven out of the Roman Empire by other people.

These nomadic people would not accept Roman rule and, by rising against the Romans, helped to contribute to the decline of the Roman Empire. The Roman roads that had been amber routes fell into poor condition, because there was no central military power that cared about maintaining the roads.

During this period—from about the third to the tenth centuries—there were many large population shifts. The Vistula Route was attacked over the centuries by peoples such as the Avars, the Slavs (who later settled in the *Slavic* countries of eastern Europe) and the

After the fall of Rome, all Europe declined; on the roads wagons such as this one were sometimes even pulled by men, rather than animals. (Bayeux tapestry, 11th century)

Magyars (who later settled in Hungary). The Brenner Pass Route was also disrupted, as wave after wave of invaders poured across it into northern Italy. Only along the Rhône-Saône Route was anything like order restored. There the Franks migrated from the lower Rhine River into the heart of Gaul. That was the beginning of the long process by which Gaul would become France.

Changing Times, Changing Travel. In all these areas, the roads suffered. Many of the old Roman highways were abandoned, and soon became filled with trees and gaping holes. Local rulers repaired some sections for regional use. For example, the Emperor Charlemagne, who ruled in France from 768 to 814, restored some of the French roads. But there was no central power to keep the whole network open, safe, and in good repair. In fact, sometimes there were good reasons *not* to have good roads—they might make it easier for invaders to travel into your country.

This is just what happened on the Brenner Pass Route. That road allowed Goths, Huns, Lombards, and others to pass through the Alps into northern Italy. In Roman times, cities had emerged along that route as travelers brought business and trade along the roads. As Rome declined, the cities often shrank to small villages. The cities that remained and grew stronger tended to be along rivers, like the Rhine or the Rhône, as people began to trade by water rather than overland.

The roads that remained quickly deteriorated and were no longer able to handle the swift chariots and fancy carriages of Roman times. Large, crude farm wagons, their heavy wooden wheels often studded with iron nails, were used to haul goods—but usually only for short distances. Over long distances the roads were simply not reliable.

Riding or walking became the main way to travel by land, as both horses and people handle bumps and holes better than wheeled vehicles do. Bulky goods like wheat might be hauled in heavy carts, but most goods were carried by caravans of pack horses or donkeys. Richer travelers rode—the poorer ones walked. As in Roman times, travelers often formed groups to protect themselves on the road. Knights or other armed riders were also hired to guard travel parties. As you can imagine, there was not much travel during these times.

This is the period of history that used to be known as the "Dark Ages." It got its name because some historians believed that the "light" of culture and civilization had gone out with the end of Roman domination. Later, historians came to understand that this period saw the flourishing of many different cultures and peoples, the ancestors of those living in Europe today.

PILGRIM TIMES

After the decline of the Roman Empire, there was no comparable, long-lasting central power in Europe. However, there was a different institution that served to connect peoples in distant regions, and that was the Catholic Church.

The Growth of Christianity. The Catholic Church grew out of the Christianity that was founded in Palestine in the first century A.D., by the followers of Jesus after his death. At first, the Christian Church was just a small group of people living in the midst of the Roman Empire. But by 313, even the Roman Emperor Constantine had converted to Christianity. This was the beginning of Christianity's association with political power.

There were many different versions of Christianity in these early days, and many struggles by people who wanted to establish their version as the "true" one. Two versions eventually squeezed out all the others: one in the East under the authority of the emperor at

Constantinople (present-day Istanbul, in modern Turkey) and one in the West under the authority of the Pope at Rome. From both centers, Christianity spread through Europe. This was a long and difficult process, as people of many different religions fought with the Christians for political power. In many areas, old religious ceremonies eventually became incorporated into Christian traditions.

In the sixth and seventh centuries, most of the peoples of Europe were Christian, at least in name, while by the end of the seventh century most of the Arab countries had converted to another religion, Islam. The split between the Eastern and the Western European versions of Christianity continued to widen, and in 1054 became more or less permanent as the Orthodox Eastern Church and the (Roman) Catholic Church.

Accepting Chritianity as their religion had an important effect on the way people saw themselves and the other people in the world. No longer were they simply residents of a local village or members of a family clan. People who considered themselves Christian saw themselves as part of *Christendom*, a huge section of the world's population.

Pilgrims and Other Travelers. As the Catholic Church established its power in Europe, trade and travel began to grow once more. Messengers, merchants, minstrels (singers and musicians), healers, couriers (message carriers), journeymen (traveling artisans), and wayfarers (travelers with no fixed home) traveled the roads in increasing numbers. Soon they were joined by another kind of traveler: the *peregrine*, or wanderer, whom we know as the *pilgrim*.

The idea of the Christian *pilgrimage* was nothing new. Then the Emperor Constantine converted to Christianity in the fourth century, Jesus's birthplace of Jerusalem came under Christian rule. Some Christians living in other places had made trips, or pilgrimages, to Jerusalem, since they considered that the land was holy.

However, as long as travel conditions remained difficult, a pilgrimage was generally undertaken only by a few dedicated people. In the 10th century, as travel became easier, pilgrimages became more popular.

Pilgrims traveled to three cities that they considered holy. Palmers went to Jerusalem, often returning with the palm branches that gave them their names. Romers went to Rome, to see the tombs of

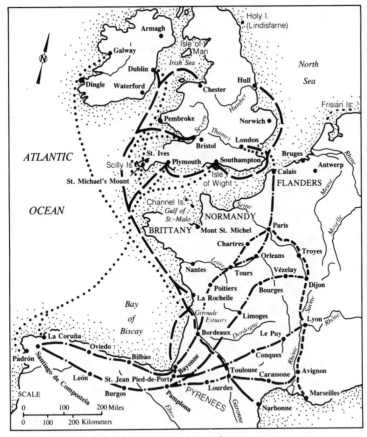

The Santiago de Compostela Routes in Medieval Times

———·———·——— Land Routes to Santiago de Compostela

············· Sea Routes to Santiago de Compostela

——— ——— ——— Tin and Wine Routes

——— ——— ——— Main Connecting Route

St. Peter and St. Paul. And those who were then called pilgrims went to Santiago de Compostela, to the Spanish tomb of the apostle St. James (*Santiago*, in Spanish).

Many of the early pilgrims were a rowdy bunch. Some had been forced to make pilgrimages as punishment for a crime. Many simply wanted an excuse to travel. Some church officials thought that pilgrimages were not quite virtuous, especially for women, who had more free contact with men than some people thought proper. Brother Felix Fabri, who made two pilgrimages to Jerusalem in the 15th century, described how order was kept on one of his journeys:

The Cathedral of St. Etienne at Toulouse was one of the shrines usually visited by pilgrims bound for Santiago de Compostela. (By A.H. Hallam Murray, *Sketches on the Old Road Through France to Florence,* 1904)

... we all decided that no more games of cards or dice should be played on board of the galley [ship], that no quarrels, swearing or blasphemies should be allowed, and that the clerks and priests should add litanies to their usual daily prayers ... for men who were gambling morning, noon and night, especially the Bishop of Orleans with his suite ...

Cathedrals and Travel Guides. Along all of the pilgrim routes people built small shrines, as well as huge cathedrals in the cities. The cathedrals were often built with very wide center aisles, so that big crowds of pilgrims could march down the center.

Both pilgrims and other travelers needed places to stay on their journeys. Inns continued to be crowded, dirty, and full of rats, mice, and other vermin. Religious orders often built *hospices,* clean, safe places for travelers to stay in and for dispensing medical care. In order to help travelers choose safe and pleasant places to stay, the first travel guides, known as *itineraries*, were circulated. Today the word *itinerary* also means "a plan of travel."

The itineraries could be quite useful. Aimery Picaud's *Guide du Pelerin* (*Guide of the Pilgrim*) warned pilgrims on the road to Santiago de Compostela about high charges extorted by the riverboatmen. He also warned that these men were so greedy that they sometimes overloaded their ferries and drowned all their passengers!

Picaud found that the toll officials in one city were greedy as well. Although they were supposed to tax only merchants, they often took money from pilgrims. According to Picaud, " ... quite frankly, they should be sent to the devil."

The First Postal Carriers. Because the pilgrims traveled far and wide, they often doubled as merchants, buying and selling goods in

Beggars, vagrants, and pilgrims were always common on the Amber Routes of Europe. (By Lucas van Leyden, 1520, Kupferstichkabinett und Sammlung der Zeichnungen, Berlin)

Merchants of the Hanseatic League, like these with their carts at Rostock, on the Baltic Sea, controlled trade on the northern Amber Routes in late medieval times. (Municipal Archives, Rostock)

towns along their routes. They also acted as private postal carriers, delivering messages and packages for officials and friends. In these days before an official postal service, people still depended on travelers to carry their letters and messages. Only the rich could afford to hire someone specially to send or pick up a message.

The Roads Improve. As travel increased, more care was given to the maintenance of the roads. Most of the roads during these medieval times were dirt paths, rougher and more difficult than the Roman roads had been. But they were adequte for travelers who mainly walked or rode—and did not care too much about dust, mud, or manure from horses and cattle.

The Growth of Trade

As merchants grew richer, they began to expand their trade. Many merchants who had shipped their goods by sea began to take their business inland, too. Naturally, they followed the main lines of the old amber routes.

One route started at the French port of Marseilles, on the Mediterranean Sea, and followed the old Rhône-Saône Route north through France, before branching off from the old amber route to become the main route across the English Channel to London.

On the Adriatic Sea, Venice became a major port. Traders carrying goods out of this major Italian city crossed the Alps through the Brenner Pass. Other routes were opening throughout Europe.

The Hanseatic League. Even those traders using the old amber routes did not take them all the way north to Denmark, or even to the German port of Hamburg. That's because this land was controlled by the Hanseatic League.

The Hanseatic League was a group of merchants in northern Germany who banded together to protect themselves from foreign competition and piracy. The Hansas—companies of merchants who traded with foreign countries—gradually joined with one another to keep other companies' goods out of their areas. They formed the Hanseatic League in 1358.

The league grew quickly, and by 1370 it had won a *monopoly* on trade in all of Scandinavia—that is, only companies who belonged to the league were allowed to do business there. This powerful organization continued to prosper for several hundred years, lasting until the 17th century.

The Hanseatic League was formed because trade had become both very profitable and very widespread. It was innovative because, when merchants organized themselves to increase profits and stifle competition, they were making a real shift from earlier trade, which was much less organized and was conducted by individuals or partnerships that were too small to affect other traders' business.

The league was so powerful that it actually prevented some outside merchants and traders not only from trading in but even from entering cities that it controlled. In the Germany city of Cologne, for example, a regulation said that any merchants who passed through Cologne on their way from certain countries could be arrested by any citizen who caught them. They would then be punished with a large fine.

However, the league did allow Italian traders to use the old Vistula Route. After so many hundreds of years, the old amber routes continued to be used.

Customs and Trade Fairs. The Hanseatic League was not the only restriction that merchants faced during this period. Many small towns and villages along the various travel routes tried to charge a customs duty on each load of goods that passed across their borders.

Merchants were especially frustrated on the Brenner Pass Route, which passed through the territory that would later become modern-day Germany, Austria, and Italy. In those days, however, Germany and German-speaking Austria were not unified nations but a group of small states, each with its own ruler, and Italy was really a collection of several small duchies (territories ruled by a duke) and city-states. Each of these small units tried to raise money by charging traveling merchants for their goods.

For example, if you were an Anglo-Saxon merchant living in northern Germany and you wanted to go to Lombardy in northern Italy, you would have to pay duties at 10 customs houses—in the Alps alone. And all conceivable goods were taxed. The regulations of one Italian town said duties were payable on "horses, male and female slaves, woolen, linen, and hemp cloth, tin, and swords." Merchants were often very angry about being charged in this way. As the regulations themselves described,

> ... when they saw their trunks and sacks being emptied at the gates, they grew angry and started rows with the employees of the treasury. The [parties] were wont to hurl abusive words and in addition very often inflicted wounds upon one another.

To solve the problem, the two regions finally made a trade agreement. The Anglo-Saxons would pay no duties and would be given safe conduct through Lombardy. In return, they would make a yearly payment of gold and other goods. Many other places along the amber routes came up with similar trade agreements. These practices—the charging of customs and the making of trade agreements—are still engaged in today.

The practice of trade fairs also continues to thrive. Trade fairs are places where people can come and do business together. Today, trade fairs mainly serve as a chance for people in a particular field, like frozen food or computers, to see everybody else's new products and learn how other businesses are doing. When they began, trade fairs were intended to give the merchants of many different nations a place where they could do business under only one standard set of taxes. Merchants from all over the world would come to the silk market at Lyons, France, or to the great trade cities of Germany's

Frankfurt-am-Main, Switzerland's Geneva, or France's Champagne. Syrian and Jewish traders from the Middle East brought silk and jewels to trade for wools and linens. International trading cities set aside special places for merchants to live in, both to protect the merchants and to make it easier for the city's government to keep an eye on them.

A Time of Disorder

The trade systems of the 13th century fell into great upheaval during the 14th century. Many factors combined to discourage both trade and travel.

Plague. One major problem was the spread of the bubonic plague, a disease that no one knew how to cure. The plague was a terrible disease that swept over Europe and Asia, killing as much as three-quarters of the population in less than 20 years. Now we have antibiotics that can help cure diseases like this and we understand that the bubonic plague was carried by fleas from infected rats. When the fleas bit the humans, the humans became sick. When the disease reached a person's lungs, they could then pass the disease on to other people through the moisture in their breathing or coughing.

In the 14th century, however, no one understood what caused the disease, so people feared many things and did not really know what to do to protect themselves. Ironically, traders and travelers on the amber route probably helped the plague to spread by carrying the infection to the places they visited. Of course, people's fear of the plague also discouraged them traveling.

Challenges to Power. Other events made travel more difficult and dangerous during the 15th and 16th centuries. This was a time of many peasant uprisings. In the feudal system of that time, peasants labored on land that belonged to a feudal lord. The lord was supposed to be responsible for the peasants by keeping an army to protect them from neighboring bandits or invaders. In exchange, the peasants were supposed to do all the farm work, providing a portion of what they produced to the lord. They were also supposed to help the lord in whatever military activities he undertook. Many peasants began to resist this system and they revolted against the upper, land-owning classes, eventually overcoming the feudal system.

Another challenge to the existing order was the rise of Protestantism in the 16th century. Many areas broke away from the Catholic Church, which at that time had great land holdings and a good deal of political power. The Protestant areas tried to reduce the Catholic Church's power by breaking up the monasteries, places where monks and other religious people lived. Many of the monastaries had large tracts of land or fertile fields, and these were seized by governments or individuals.

Naturally, without monasteries there were almost no hospices, and travelers were once again without safe places to stay along their routes. With the weakening of the Catholic Church, there were also fewer pilgrimages, although many religious Catholics still traveled to Rome.

In addition, the contest between Catholics and Protestants was a very bitter one. Not only religious questions were at stake—people from the two religious groups were also struggling over the political control of the areas they lived in. The wars and fighting this created made land travel difficult and dangerous, with the result that more and more traders turned to the sea as a safer way to travel.

New Expectations. Ironically, even as travel conditions were getting worse, people were becoming more demanding. Earlier travelers had been satisfied to walk or to ride a horse. But many Europeans of the 16th century wanted to travel by carriage.

Across the great rivers of northern Europe, ferries have operated for thousands of years, like this one on the Vistula. (By Daniel Chodowicki, 1773, Kupferstichkabinett und Sammlung der Zeichnungen, Berlin)

Critics of the roads of that time were surely in contempt of them. On many routes, the bridle path beside the route was in better shape than the road itself. The wooden bridges across many streams could not be trusted, and the corduroy roads were not well maintained. Toll ferries and fords were the only means of crossing rivers that were trusted. In many parts of eastern Europe, the main road was simply a beaten path through the middle of a forest.

If a passenger of that time wanted to be safe rather than sorry, he or she had to carry large planks and loads of twigs to be sure of getting the carriage out of the inevitable mudholes. Coach passengers might have to help the driver haul their vehicle out of the mud. They had to face the possibility of being overturned into a stream or a snowbank. The carriage might break down, requiring passengers to stand for hours by the roadside while the coachman or local blacksmith tried to fix a broken wheel or axle.

Not only was their travel slow and inconvenient—it was also expensive. And it hurt! Since there were almost no springs in the carriages of that time, each bump on the road meant a bruise for the passengers. One German writer said that no one should ride in a carriage unless he or she had "a breast of iron, innards of copper and a posterior of platinum."

THE DEVELOPMENT OF THE POSTAL SYSTEM

In medieval times, there was no regular messenger service. Kings, bishops, and rich merchants had private couriers, people whom they paid to carry messages for them. As we saw, pilgrims and other travelers might carry messages or packages, but this was not a very reliable way of ensuring delivery. As trade grew between different parts of Europe, and as political issues expanded to include more than just the neighboring village, it became more and more important to have a systematic, organized way of getting information to and from other parts of the world.

The First Postal Service. By the 16th century, a better postal system was becoming a necessity as the volume and demand for communication to distant places increased. An early attempt at one was made by Maximilian I, a German emperor and king who tried to expand his rule by marrying himself and his children to people with huge holdings of their own. When he wanted to build a new postal service, Maximilian called on the Taxis family of Venice, since

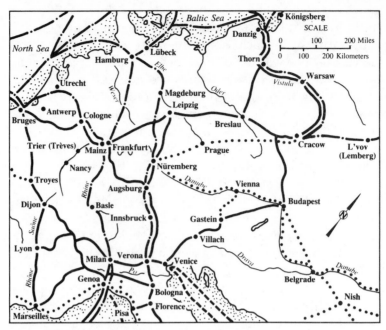

The Amber Routes in Late Medieval Times

———————— Main Italian Trade Routes

—·——·——·— Main Hanseatic Trade Routes

• • • • • • • • Other Main Land Routes

— — — — — — Other Main Sea Routes

the Taxis had been running one of the best private courier services in Europe since the 14th century.

The Taxis used a series of relay posts. A rider would go from one post to the next, where he would pass his packages on to a new rider with a fresh horse. The riders carried messages in a sealed pouch, to protect their privacy.

At first, the riders carried only royal messages. But the couriers soon began to carry private "mail" as well. This system was so successful that it spread throughout Europe. A single traveler could journey only about 20 miles in one day, before having to rest both himself and his horses. But a postal relay, using several riders and horses, could travel as much as 100 miles a day, depending on the weather.

The Taxis family ran the main postal system in central Europe for over three centuries. But other postal systems grew up alongside it. A mail pouch might travel through more than one postal system before it reached its destination.

Even after roads had been improved, 19th-century travelers often preferred to walk or ride than to hazard stagecoaches on narrow passes like St. Gotthard. (From F. Schoppe and C. W. Gropius, *Malerische Ansichten Gegenden ... auf einer Reise durch Oesterreich ... und Unteritalien,* 1823–1825, Germanisches Nationalmuseum, Nuremberg)

THE BEGINNINGS OF TOURISM

Mail Coaches and Their Passengers. Later, mail began to be carried in a coach, rather than by a single rider. Gradually, mail coaches began to carry passengers. By the so-called *post-chaise system*, passengers could travel all the way across Europe.

Mail coaches were still very slow. Roads were in a terrible condition and coaches would usually stop overnight. Even so, Europeans were ready to travel. Now that travelers did not have to own coaches, travel along the amber routes increased once again. Now the aim was not necessarily to make a pilgrimage or to do do business, but sometimes just to see the world.

Travel was still long and hard. Most travelers were worried enough about what might happen that they put their affairs in order and made a will before leaving on their trips! A journey might last several months, which was expensive, especially when you added up the coach fares, the inn expenses, and the heavy tolls to pay at every border. This was especially hard on young journeymen, workers who journeyed from place to place in order to work their trades. Because people still faced plagues and diseases, travelers were required to have health certificates. Sometimes they were held in *quarantine*, or confinement, for 40 days or more, just to make sure they weren't sick—even if they already had health certificates.

Travel Improvements. Through all the hardships, travel continued and even expanded. And eventually, in the 18th century, roads were finally improved. Travel time was cut in half in many places when this happened. Not only were the old amber routes improved, but comfortable inns were also built alongside them, especially in western Germany and Austria.

Roads and conditions were far worse in eastern Germany and Poland. There was simply a pair of ruts cut by an axle into the mud. If your carriage's wheels weren't exactly as far apart as the ruts, you couldn't travel on the road at all and would have to use the field beside it. Instead of a comfortable inn, you might find a stable for horses—with the passengers expected to sleep on straw beside the beasts.

Conditions continued to improve in the 19th century, as rich young men began making the so-called "Grand Tour" of the Continent—a leisurely trip lasting a year or more to see all the famous places of Europe. Even people from the middle classes began traveling for pleasure instead of simply for business. This is the time when the word *tourist* was first formed—because it was the first time in history when large numbers of people traveled, or "toured," for pleasure.

In Eastern Europe, travelers were often obliged to sleep in public rooms on pallets of straw. (By Daniel Chodowicki, 1773, Kupferstichkabinett und Sammlung der Zeichnungen, Berlin)

This 1842 illustration well conveys the amount of pushing, walking, and just plain waiting involved in stagecoach traveling. (From Jean Grandeville, *Die kleinen Leiden des menschlichen Lebens)*

It was also the first time that "nature" was seen as an object of beauty that was worth visiting for its own sake. The Alps were no longer just an obstacle to cross. Now they became tourist attractions that people traveled to just to look at.

The British invented the *express post*, coaches that traveled both night and day, changing horses and drivers while the passengers slept. This made travel much faster, allowing people to plan shorter trips.

Yet people still complained about the problems of travel. Diplomat Alexander von Villers wrote:

> This rushing from place to place, pack, unpack, get tickets, change carriage, inns with impertinent dandified waiters, terrible food, marrow-chilling bills, robbery without sword or pistol, money, money, always money, nothing but money—what must one be like to endure all that? Let nobody talk to me about the joy of that kind of travel. I don't believe in it.

One response to complaints like Villers' was the development of the package tour, an idea that is still with us today. For one lump sum, a traveler could purchase a whole trip, with all the arrange-

The arrival of a stagecoach—this one is called a *diligence*—was always an occasion for bustle; written on the building at the rear is a list of towns visited by the coach service. (From a painting by L. L. Boilly, 18th century, authors' archives)

ments made. This arrangement was especially popular with timid, first-time travelers who wanted to be sure of safe and "respectable" lodgings.

PLANES, TRAINS, AND AUTOMOBILES

After the age of coach travel came the railroad. Iron rails pushed through marshes and mountains, linking Europe as never before and changing its character forever. And after the railroad came the automobile. Today, concrete highways cut through the modern nations of Europe, and the cars traveling on them race by with a speed undreamed-of thousands of years ago.

Parts of all three amber routes still survive, but only the Rhône-Saône Route remains in anything like its original form—a highway running from north Germany south in two branches, to France and Italy.

The Brenner Pass is still the easiest route through the Alps. But the border between East Germany and West Germany blocks travelers from its old course north to Denmark. The Vistula Route has also been affected by the political differences that divide Austria, Czechoslovakia, and Poland.

When the amber routes were first formed, Europe counted on the Mediterranean to communicate with the rest of the world. The lure of ships docked at Venice and Marseilles carrying goods from the East was part of the inspiration for trade along the routes that ran from those major ports up to remote parts of northern Europe.

Now airplanes overshadow the land and sea routes and northern Europe itself is the dog that wags the tail of trade. Nevertheless, the amber routes can still be traced, and Europeans are proud of their heritage. Many an amateur archaeologist in northern Europe will tell you proudly, "I live on the amber route!"

SUGGESTIONS FOR FURTHER READING

Bautier, Robert-Henri. *The Economic Development of Medieval Europe* (London: Thames and Hudson, 1971).

Braudel, Fernand. *The Wheels of Commerce* (New York: Harper & Row, 1982). Volume 2 of *Civilization and Capitalism, 15th–18th Century*, translated from the French by Siân Reynolds.

Chevallier, Raymond. *Roman Roads* (Berkeley and Los Angeles: University of California Press, 1976). Translated by N. H. Field.

Clark, J. G. D. *Prehistoric Europe: The Economic Basis* (London: Methuen, 1974; reprint of 1952 edition).

de Navarro, J. M. "Prehistoric Routes Between Northern Europe and Italy Defined by the Amber Trade," *The Geographical Journal*, Vol. 66, No. 6, December 1925.

East, W. Gordon. *An Historical Geography of Europe, Third Edition* (London: Methuen, 1948).

Heichelheim, Fritz M. *An Ancient Economic History: From the Paleolithic Age to the Migrations of the Germanic, Slavic and Arabic Nations*, in three volumes (Leyden: A. W. Sijthoff, vols. 1 & 2, 1968; vol. 3, 1970). Translated into English by Joyce Stevens.

Hindley, Geoffrey. *A History of Roads* (Secaucus, New Jersey: Citadel Press, 1972).

Kendall, Alan. *Medieval Pilgrims* (New York: Putnam, 1970). Part of the Putnam Documentary History Series.

Leighton, Alan. *Transport and Communication in Early Medieval Europe, A.D. 500–1100* (Newton Abbot: David & Charles, 1972).

Loschburg, Winfried. *A History of Travel* (London: George Prior Associated Publishers Ltd., Edition Leipzig, 1979).

Merrick, Hugh. *The Great Motor Highways of the Alps* (London: Robert Hale, Ltd., 1958).

Piggott, Stuart. *Ancient Europe: From the Beginnings of Agriculture to Classical Antiquity* (Chicago: Aldine, 1965).

Pliny the Elder. *Natural History*, in 10 volumes (Cambridge, Massachusetts: Harvard University Press, 1938). Part of the Loeb Classical Library. Translated by H. Rackham.

Pounds, Norman J. G. *An Historical Geography of Europe, 450 B.C.–A.D. 1330* (New York: Cambridge University Press, 1973) and *An Historical Geography of Europe, 1500–1840* (New York: Cambridge University Press, 1980).

Shreiber, Hermann. *The History of Roads: From Amber Route to Motorway* (London: Barrie and Rockliff, 1961). Translated from the German by Stewart Thomson.

Von Hagen, Victor W. *The Roads That Led to Rome* (Cleveland and New York: World, 1967).

Zilliacus, Laurin. *Mail for the World: From the Courier to the Universal Postal Union* (New York: John Day, 1953).

2
THE APPIAN WAY AND THE EGNATIAN WAY

THE ROADS TO POWER

For many hundreds of years, the greatest power in Europe was the Roman Empire. Starting as a tiny city built on seven hills along the Tiber River, Rome went on to conquer peoples throughout most of Europe and even in the Near Eastern portion of Asia.

The Romans conquered foreign peoples with their large armies, and continued to rule with their system of military and political leadership. In order to get and keep power, they depended on their famous roads. They needed roads for soldiers to march on, for couriers to carry messages to and from governors in outlying areas, and for traders to intermingle the economies of Rome and its subject states.

The two key roads of the Roman Empire were the *Appian Way* and the *Egnatian Way*. The Appian Way (in Latin, the *Via Appia*) was the road that first bound the many different peoples of Italy into the Roman state. When the empire expanded to the east, the Via Appia was joined to the Egnatian Way (the *Via Egnatia*) through a short sea connection across the Adriatic. The two roads formed the "Great East Road" from Rome to the Empire's second capital at Byzantium (a city later renamed *Constantinople* and now called *Istanbul*, in modern Turkey).

Looking at the history of the Appian and the Egnatian Ways is one method of understanding the growth in power of the Roman Empire. Later, after the empire fell and other powers expanded to take its place, the Appian and Egnatian Ways played a role in their

The Appian Way and Egnatian Way in Roman Times

—·—·—·— Via Appia   ········· Main Connecting Land Routes

-------- Via Appia Traiana   ———— Appia-Egnatia Sea Connection

———— Via Egnatia

stories, too. To help us understand who has held power in the western world, we can turn to the stories of these two great roads.

ROME BEFORE THE ROADS

Early Myths and Legends. There are two remotely connected stories about the founding of Rome. One was created out of myth and legend in the great epic poem, the *Aeneid*, written by the Roman poet Virgil. The *Aeneid* is the story of Aeneas, who was the legendary son of the goddess Venus and the mortal man Anchises. Aeneas was a Trojan who escaped from the burning city with his goddess-mother's help when Troy fell to the Greeks at the end of the Trojan War. He wandered from Troy (in present-day Turkey) to Carthage (in present-day Tunisia) to Italy. Many years later, according to Virgil, his descendants founded Rome.

At the later time, according to a legend more traditional in Virgil's time, the war god Mars (whom the Greeks called Ares) had twin sons by a mortal woman named Rhea Silvia. Rhea was the daughter of a king who had been thrown out of power. The man who threw her father out did not want her children to live, so he threw them into the Tiber River. Instead of drowning, the two babies floated ashore, where they were found by a she-wolf, who nursed them and saved their lives. Later, they were raised by a shepherd, who named them Romulus and Remus. When the boys grew up, they killed the man who had stolen the throne and put their grandfather back into power. Then they founded a city on the spot where they were rescued from the Tiber. But the two brothers quarreled and fought to the death. Romulus killed Remus and named the city after himself—*Rome*. He ruled the city for many years, but then, instead of dying like a human king, he was supposed to have vanished in a thunderstorm.

No matter how it happened, historians agree that Rome was founded some time around 753 B.C. At this time, the Italian peninsula was still the home of many small tribes. Meanwhile, farther east, the peoples around the Aegean Sea were developing an elaborate culture.

Greeks took products like wine and oil, in containers like these, into the regions north of them, helping to open up the Egnatian Way. (Greek Government Department of Information)

Building the First Road. The cultural life around the Aegean Sea included many early traders, who traveled back and forth between Troy and the city-states of Greece. They were the first people who made this trip, and so had to beat the trail themselves. Often they had to work their way through a maze of mountains, trying and abandoning one dead end after another. When they found a trail that was adequate, they had to physically clear a space wide enough for a person to pass. This pathway was the beginning of the Egnatian Way.

The route was a battleground for many centuries. Greeks from the south fought over the territory with Persians (ancestors of today's Iranians) from Asia Minor. Later, the Macedonians (ancestors of a people in today's Greece, Bulgaria, and Yugoslavia) ruled over both the Persians and the Greeks. Still later, the Celts (who eventually settled in today's Ireland) tried to seize power as well. Not until the Roman Empire would one people finally succeed in seizing and holding power in that region for any length of time.

The Growth of Rome

In 500 B.C., Rome was just a small walled city, like many others in Italy. At that time, many different peoples had settled in Italy. All of them admired the site of Rome: its seven hills were easy to defend, the water of the Tiber was sweet and drinkable, and the river valley led easily down to the sea, where salt was available.

But the peoples of Italy could agree on little else. In our own day, with Italy functioning as a unified nation, it is sometimes difficult to remember that the ancestors of the present-day Italians were many different peoples, who for many years lived quite separately from one another, speaking different languages and practicing different customs. These ancestors include the Etruscans, who lived in the north; the Illyrians on the east coast; the Italics in the central part of the peninsula; and the Greeks, who had several colonies around the heel of Italy's boot and in Sicily.

Ironically, these different peoples did not come together until they faced a threat from outside. When the Celts invaded from the north in the fourth century B.C., the peoples of central Italy formed a Latin League for their common defense. Rome gradually became the strongest city in the league, and within decades had conquered most of the peoples in central Italy.

Building the Roads

One famous Roman, Appius Claudius, decided that Rome should push through central Italy to conquer the peoples in the south. He believed that the first step in Rome's expansion was to build a road to the south and east. This was a natural step for him to take, from his position as head of the city's public works. (He was also the censor in charge of public morals!) In 312 B.C. Appius Claudius began building the road that would be named after him—the Via Appia, or Appian Way.

The Romans had few models to follow. Up until then, sea routes had been the main method of travel in this region. Roads were not made or built—they were mere trails beaten through forests or fields. The Appian Way was the first road that the Romans built, and on it they learned the skills that they would later use on the roads they built throughout the rest of their empire.

Engineering Problems. Appius Claudius began with a footpath that had been beaten down over earlier centuries. He sent engineers and laborers—many of them convicted prisoners sentenced to hard labor—to widen and clear the old route.

One big engineering problem was drainage. Roads had to be built in such a way that water would run off them when it rained, rather than soak through the road and turn everything to mud and puddles. Claudius's workers built drainage ditches and curbing on the roadside, and built up the center of the road to help water to run off.

The engineers also tried to keep the road as level as possible. At the same time, they tried to stay on the slopes of valleys, rather than build at valley bottoms, where water would have no place to run off.

The workers faced a similar problem when the road had to run across, instead of down, a valley. If they let the road follow the

South of Rome, the Appian Way ran in a straight line through this little village, with the Alban Mountains in the distance. (From James Henry Breasted, *Ancient Times: A History of the Early World ...*, 1914)

valley's shape, curving down and then up again, water would naturally run down to collect at the bottom of the roadway. In addition, it is more difficult to travel on a road that curves up and down than on a road that is level. The road workers solved this problem by building a kind of bridge on linked stone arches, called a *viaduct*, which created a level road from slope to slope, across the top of a valley.

Marshes posed a more difficult problem, especially the 10-mile-wide Pontine Marshes. In earlier times, ferries had crossed the marshes through canals. Although the ferries continued to run, the Romans also built a causeway across the marshes, a kind of road supported on piles (or pillars) driven deep into the mud.

Bridges were also needed to cross rivers and streams. In this early period, most bridges were built out of wood, but later bridges would be made of stone.

The Roman builders tried to avoid sharp curves, since the clumsy wagons of this time had trouble making tight turns. If a road had to pass through a mountainous area, the builders might have to cut sections of rock out of the mountain to make it easier for wagons to pass. But when it was necessary, they might have to curve the road around the barrier instead.

The great Roman roads and highways were paved with specially cut solid blocks of stone; in towns, as here in ancient Pompeii, stepping stones were also provided, so walkers would not have to step in puddles on rainy days. (From James Henry Breasted, *Ancient Times: A History of The Early World ...*, 1914)

The width of the road also varied, depending on the country and the type of traffic expected on the route. Some parts of the Appian Way were as wide as 10 to 15 feet—but some parts were only eight feet across. Much later, when traffic became heavier, the Romans developed fixed standards for their roads, but in this early time, people were grateful to have any sort of road at all.

At this time, paved roads were almost unknown. The road surface itself might be beaten dirt or, in an especially wet area, a few wooden logs set across the marsh. Claudius Appius had a different idea. The first section of his road—the 132 miles from Rome to the city of Capua—was originally covered with gravel. And the very first mile of the road, which led to the Temple of Mars on the outskirts of the city, was paved with cut stone. Later, in 295 B.C., Roman engineers began to use heavy cut blocks of volcanic rock—*silex*—as the base of their roads.

Extending the Road. The building of the Via Appia went on over several decades as the road was extended across the peninsula to Hydruntum, at the head of the Ionian Sea. In the coastal area the workers often had less heavy construction to do. The region had an underlying layer of dry bedrock hard enough and close enough to the surface to serve as the base for the road. Workers had only to clear away the undergrowth and the loose rocks, and then build drainage ditches. By about the middle of the third century B.C., the Romans had completed the Via Appia.

BATTLING ON THE APPIAN WAY

The Romans did not get all the way to the sea without a fight. When they reached the territory of the Samnite people, they stopped and built a fort. Then they brought in soldiers to guard their road builders while they extended the road. The road made it easier to bring in more troops. Later, Roman colonists would use the road to settle in these conquered lands.

But roads can serve enemies, as well. Two famous enemies of Rome used the Appian Way and almost defeated the Romans.

King Pyrrhus and His Victory. In 281 B.C., King Pyrrhus of Epiros—a country in northwestern Greece—came to the aid of a besieged ally city, Tarentum, which had ruled the lands around the city of Capua. Pyrrhus's soldiers and the soldiers of this southern

Italian state fought against Roman soldiers, back and forth along the Appian Way. Pyrrhus actually won two important battles, but his losses were so heavy that he is supposed to have said, "One more victory like this and I am lost." Today we have a phrase, *Pyrrhic victory*, which means a victory that costs more than it is worth. Eventually Pyrrhus went back to Epiros, leaving the Romans to rule southern Italy.

Hannibal and His Elephants. Another general who fought Rome was Hannibal, the ruler of Carthage in northern Africa. (Carthage was an ancient city near the site of modern-day Tunis, in Tunisia.) Hannibal is considered one of the greatest military geniuses of all time. At the middle of the third century B.C., he set out to invade Italy with a small group of carefully selected soldiers. Hannibal's plan was to cross the Alps, using his African elephants to carry his army's equipment. Having successfully crossed the mountains, Hannibal headed south into Italy and gained control of the Via Appia at the city of Sinuessa.

Hannibal used his control of the road to cut off Rome's food supplies from the south. The Romans tried to box Hannibal in, fortifying a river crossing and a mountain pass to trap him. But Hannibal broke out of the trap. He came back the next year to cut off the road again—at the city of Capua.

Hannibal had one obstacle that he could not overcome. He was in unfriendly country, cut off from his own supplies across the Mediter-

Children of wealthy Roman families had their own chariots drawn by a small animal, like this one enshrined in stone. (Louvre)

This is a 19th-century reconstruction of the Appian Way. (By Canina, German Archaeological Institute, Rome)

ranean. Finally he, like Pyrrhus, was forced to retreat from Italy. When he left in 202 B.C., Rome regained control of the Appian Way.

LIFE ALONG THE APPIAN WAY

With Hannibal and his Carthaginian army gone, Rome began to use the Appian Way once again to extend its power into southern Italy. Rome sent out colonists to rebuild the towns along the Way that had been damaged in the fighting, and to found new towns. Many towns grew up around inns or public houses, places along the road where a weary traveler or an official courier could get a meal and a bed for the night.

Imagine the traffic along the Appian Way at this time. Walking down the road, you might see a trader carrying silks from the east or furs from the north, heading for the profitable markets of Rome. A troupe of wandering actors might be discussing the play they hoped to present in the big city, while a teacher of Greek and a philosopher discussed whether anyone in Rome would hire their services. The larger and more powerful Rome grew, the more people were attracted to the city.

The Road Improves. As the power of Rome increased, the city could afford to send more workers to improve the surrounding roads. And as Rome became more secure, it could dispense with temporary bridges that could be pulled up or boat bridges that could be pulled apart in case of invasion. Now Rome wanted permanent bridges and secure roads. In the second century B.C., the Romans began building heavy stone bridges instead of wooden ones. Many of these solid stone structures were so well built that they are still standing today. They had to be strong to support the heavily loaded wagons that brought food to the fast-growing city.

ROME GOES EAST

With its home base secure, Rome looked across the Adriatic Sea. Troops were sent into Macedonia, Thrace, and Asia Minor, eventually conquering huge portions of these eastern lands. As they had done with the Via Appia, the Romans began to build a road out of the rough track they found, in order to consolidate their military and political power.

The 500-mile route eventually became known as the Via Egnatia. No one knows the source of the name, although some speculate that one of the main builders was called Ignatius, or Egnatius.

A New Military Road. Even after they took Macedonia, the Romans had to fight the free mountain peoples along the Via Egnatia, which thus began as a primarily military road. Macedonia had always been full of free and independent-minded peoples, so that, as the Roman writer Cicero said, even its own governors "have always held that the boundaries extend only as far as swords and javelins can reach."

The Romans followed their military triumphs by carving the region into Roman provinces. But throughout the second century B.C. and into the first, the Romans continued to fight the mountain peoples.

Engineering Improvements. The builders of the Via Egnatia had learned well from their experience on other Roman roads. This new highway had a curved base or *camber*, high in the center to help the water run off into the drainage ditches on either side. Construction was economical: the earth dug out of the drainage ditches was used to build up the road's center. The road was also bordered by curbs.

In most places, the Via Egnatia was nine to twelve feet wide—that is, wide enough for wagons to pass each other. In rocky mountain

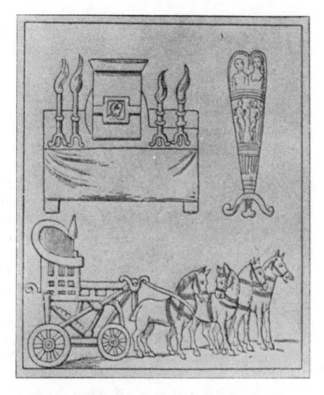

This badge of a fourth-century Roman governor on the Egnatian Way quite naturally includes a four-horse chariot. (New York Public Library)

passes, however, the road was only six feet wide, cut along the old mountain tracks. And near some cities, the road was as wide as 36 feet. Imagine the early traffic jams that had to be avoided!

The Via Egnatia had some of the first billboards. Milestones were set up every 1,000 paces to give the distance between cities. But these markers also advertised the builders, sponsors and, later, the repairers of the road.

One further innovation made this road more convenient to horseback riders: mounting stones. A rider standing on one of these stones could more easily mount a horse. These stones were necessary because stirrups were not yet in use.

Some parts of this road still exist. And if you look at the soft limestone surface in some places, you can still see the tracks of wheels from thousands of years ago.

REBELS AND SLAVES

Some people in Rome prospered from this expansion. But others remained poor and were badly treated. Many people in Roman colonies felt that they could not afford to pay the heavy taxes demanded by the Roman government. People from these areas faced an additional hardship: They might be taken and sold as slaves.

At various times in Roman history, slaves and dissatisfied colonists rebelled against what they felt was the unjust Roman system. In the first and second centuries B.C., there were three major slave revolts. The most famous of these revolts was the last, led by a slave named Spartacus.

Spartacus was a *gladiator*, a man who fought wild animals or other men to the death for the amusement of people who came to watch the fighting. Spartacus rebelled at this treatment and organized a band of other slaves around Capua in southern Italy, where he had been forced to train at a gladiator school.

Spartacus was soon joined by tens of thousands of volunteers, showing that many slaves were willing to risk their lives to fight for freedom against Roman rule. This rebel army marched north on the Appian Way, heading for freedom beyond the Alps. Later, Spartacus's army changed its plans and turned south again, hoping to sail to Sicily or Africa. But their sea connections failed. Although they had defeated the Roman army in several earlier battles, they were themselves finally defeated.

The punishment that the Romans dealt out was severe, because the Romans understood that if slaves believed they could revolt without punishment, they would continue to rebel and to fight for their freedom. Spartacus and many others died in battle. But 6,000 of the slaves who had fought with him were crucified along the Appian Way.

CIVIL WAR IN ROME

While the Roman government was fighting mountain peoples in Macedonia and slaves in southern Italy, it was also engaged in in-fighting. Factional struggles for control of the government of Rome would eventually lead to many years of civil war. The war began with the conflict between two Roman politicians, Julius Caesar and Pompey.

Caesar and Pompey. Ironically, Caesar and Pompey had begun as allies. When Caesar was just a minor politician, he had helped Pompey, his son-in-law, obtain supreme command of the army fighting in the East. At this time, Rome was still a republic; that is, many offices were elected and a Senate and other bodies shared political power. Caesar would soon change all this.

In 60 B.C., Caesar joined with Pompey and Crassus to form the first *triumvirate*—a group of three men that ruled Rome. Caesar went on to conquer Gaul—now France—and defeat the Britons in battle. Pompey and Crassus had earlier put down Spartacus's revolt.

Then Crassus died in 53 B.C., leaving only Caesar and Pompey. When Pompey ordered Caesar to disband the army he had used to conquer France, Caesar refused. He mobilized his soldiers in the province of Cisalpine Gaul, and then crossed the Rubicon River to enter the Italian heartland and fight Pompey. His action is the source of the phrase, "crossing the Rubicon," which means taking a decisive step from which there is no turning back.

After Caesar crossed the Rubicon, Pompey fled down the Via Appia to the town of Brundisium (today, Brindisi). Pompey wanted to capture Macedonia and the East, to strengthen his army. Caesar quickly took control of the western provinces and Italy—and the Via Appia. Then he headed east himself.

Caesar used the Via Egnatia to send an urgent messenger to Pompey, proposing negotiations. Pompey would not negotiate and thus the armies fought. Caesar had been joined by the army of his loyal colleague, Mark Antony.

But the fight between Caesar and Pompey took a long time to resolve. Both armies advanced eastward, sometimes on the Egnatia, sometimes on other roads. Finally, Caesar defeated Pompey in Greece in 48 B.C. Pompey retreated to Egypt, where he was killed, and Caesar went east to win more territories for the Roman Empire. When he returned home, a victory parade was given in his honor, such as no Roman general had ever before been given.

Assassination and Betrayal. Caesar's great powers aroused resentment in his enemies and even among some of his friends, including the politicians Brutus and Cassius. This resentment brought about his assassination in 44 B.C. Popular feeling forced Brutus and Cassius and the other assassins to leave Rome. However, some of them were given offices abroad.

Brutus and Cassius were not satisfied. From their bases in Asia, they began to raise money for an army and a fleet of ships. They were planning to attack the rule of Marc Antony and Caesar's nephew Octavian, who were part of a new triumvirate governing Rome.

To head off the rebel army, Antony and Octavian sent their army across the Appian Way, onto the Egnatian Way. They knew that the only way that Brutus and Cassius could get to Rome was by these great routes. The two sides met in their final battle, the battle of Philippi, in 42 B.C. When Brutus and Cassius's side lost, both men committed suicide.

Antony and Cleopatra. But the civil war was still not over. Some 10 years later, Mark Antony and the Egyptian Queen Cleopatra tried to seize power for themselves. When they were defeated (the subject of Shakespeare's *Antony and Cleopatra*), Octavian was left to rule alone, under the name of Caesar Augustus. The Roman Republic was now completely over: the rule of the Roman emperors had begun. And for some 200 years, the Via Appia and the Via Egnatia would be controlled by Rome without an outside challenge.

THE YEARS OF EMPIRE

Now that Rome controlled such huge territories without fear of invasion, travel increased. People could travel for thousands of miles and still be within the Roman Empire.

Travel was heaviest around Rome itself. Just as many people go on vacations today, so people tried to get out of Rome for the summer if they possibly could. The city was extremely hot in summer, and the danger of malaria from mosquitoes breeding in the swamps was greatest at this time.

Many of the wealthy classes had country *villas*, or homes, north or south of the city. Some people even commuted 20 to 25 miles into the city each day. Roman roads made this kind of travel possible.

Long-distance travel into and out of Rome also increased, especially on the Appian and Egnatian Ways. Many people wanted to seek their fortunes—or their pleasure—in the giant city of Rome.

Imagine what the Appian and Egnatian Ways must have been like in those times. By day, the roads would be crowded with *litters* (covered cots or platforms on which rich people rode; they were carried by servants, slaves, or animals), chariots, and horse-drawn carriages. A swift rider carrying an urgent message might try frantically to guide his horse through the traffic jam of these who could only afford to go on foot. Perhaps these pedestrians included a country boy seeking his fortune, dreaming about the wealth he could win in the big city. Walking beside him might be a troupe of

traveling actors planning their next production, a doctor musing about how to find wealthy Roman patients, a traveling artisan thinking about how he would set up a small shop to make and sell his amber jewelry.

At night, the road would be crowded with hundreds of heavy carts, rolling into the city with food and other supplies to sell at market the next day. Traffic was such a problem that wheeled vehicles were forbidden inside the city during the day. Some cities today have similar traffic regulations!

Many travelers put on a huge show to impress others. More than one rich young man spent his inheritance making a great show of wealth on the road—and then had to join the army when he ran out of money. Others did the opposite, faking poverty or disaster in order to fool robbers. The writer Seneca boasted that he traveled as if he had been shipwrecked, although his actual description of his travels does not make him sound very deprived. He said he traveled "with very few slaves—one carriage load—and no paraphernalia ... The mattress lives upon the ground, and I upon the mattress."

Highwaymen usually looked for isolated places in which to trap travelers and steal their goods. Some highwaymen became popular heroes. Like Italian Robin Hoods, they had the reputation of stealing from the rich to give to the poor. The robber Felix Bulla had a

Alongside the Appian Way and other major roads were aqueducts bringing water to Rome, mostly underground but near the city carried high on heavy pillars, as these ruins show. (From James Henry Breasted, *Ancient Times: A History of The Early World ...*, 1914)

Activity at a Roman coastal post-station—with mail coach, two-wheeled chariot, mounted horseman, and freighter—is detailed in this 19th-century drawing. (By Ludwig Burger)

network of hundreds of people helping him, telling him where and how to find likely people to rob. Bulla told the Romans quite clearly why, in his opinion, robbery was so widespread: "If masters treated their slaves better, there would be no robbers." When Bulla was finally captured, he was thrown to the lions in one of the bloody circuses of the Roman Empire.

Horace's Story. One of the best pictures of Roman travel in those days is given by the Roman poet Horace, who traveled south on the Appian Way toward the city of Brundisium (Brindisi). Stopping first at "a modest inn at Aricia," he found Forum Appii "crammed with boatmen and stingy tavernkeepers."

Horace commented that "the Appian Way is less tiring, if taken slowly." There is no doubt about that, for carriages in those days had no springs. The hard and somewhat uneven stone surface of the road was surely painful to travelers. Litters—covered cots carried by people or animals—were popular with those being carried because the bearers were the ones who absorbed the shocks and bumps of the road.

Horace paints a vivid picture of crossing the Pontine Marshes at night:

> Then slaves loudly rail at boatmen, boatmen at slaves, "Bring to here!" "You're packing in hundreds!" "Stay, that's enough!" What with collecting fares and harnessing the mule, a whole hour slips away. Cursed gnats and frogs of the fens drive off sleep, the boatman, soaked in sour wine, singing the while of the girl he left behind, and a passenger taking up the refrain. The passenger at last tires and falls asleep, and the lazy boatman turns his mule out to graze, ties the reins to a stone, and drops a-snoring on his back. Day was now dawning when we find our craft was not under way, until one hot-headed fellow jumps out, and with willow cudgel bangs mule and boatman on back and head.

Like many other Roman travelers, Horace detoured off the main route of the Via Appia to visit friends. Sometimes, though, he stayed at wayside inns, like the one at the city of Beneventum:

> … where our bustling host was nearly burned out while turning lean thrushes [a kind of songbird that was also good to eat] over the fire. For as Vulcan [the god of fire] slipped out through the old kitchen, the vagrant flame hastened to lick the roof. Then you might have seen the hungry guests and frightened slaves snatching up the dinner, and all trying to quench the blaze.

When Horace finally reached his destination, he was exhausted by the long days of travel. He ends his story by saying, "Brundisium is the end of a long story and of a long journey."

THE IMPORTANCE OF LAND ROUTES

As Rome continued to expand to the East, Brundisium became an ever more important port. Travelers reached the eastern Mediterranean through this port, which thus connected sea routes to the land route of the Appian Way. But although ships were fine for long distances and in good weather, the Mediterranean was not safe in late autumn and winter. And at all times of year, winds were uncertain, so that the sea routes often took longer than land travel.

The Egnatian Way, on the other hand, was a very reliable route east. Travel in the mountain passes was rarely stopped, even by snow, for more than a week or two at a time. When Caesar Augustus set up an imperial postal service to carry messages to and from his eastern colonies, his couriers rode along the Egnatian Way. This was also the main route for soldiers.

The Roman Empire was held together by soldiers and officials like this one, riding out to bring Roman control to even the remotest province. (Authors' archives)

The Egnatian Way was especially important to Augustus in his campaign against the Balkan ancestors of the modern people of Yugoslavia. Augustus wanted both to conquer these people in battle and to colonize the area, both of which plans required sending in soldiers along the way.

THE COMING OF CHRISTIANITY

The founding of Christianity was the beginning of a new world religion. It also signaled a later, major political change for the Roman Empire.

Christianity is the religion of those who consider Jesus to be the *Christ*, the son of God. This religion began in the eastern part of the Roman Empire, where Jesus lived and died. Jesus's *apostles*, or followers, traveled throughout the eastern part of the empire, frequently using the Egnatian Way. The Bible's Book of Acts (16:9-12) describes the Christian preacher Paul's journey to the city of Philippi in Macedonia (in present-day Greece). That is the city where Paul and his colleague Silas were bound in jail—and freed by one of the region's many earthquakes.

At first, the Roman government saw the Christians as dangerous political opponents who were challenging the foundations of the empire. Christians who had been born as Roman citizens were often sent in to fight lions at the bloody circuses of Rome. Others were forced to work at the post-stations (places where couriers could stop, rest, and change horses) along the Roman road system, especially along the wild and unsettled parts of the Via Egnatia.

Ironically, the very power that helped make Rome strong—its roads—also helped weaken it. Despite the oppression they faced, these early Christians found strength by keeping in touch, which they could do partly through Roman roads. So long as couriers traveled between them, groups hundreds of miles apart could stay in contact. Indeed, some Christians worked as volunteer messengers, carrying letters between communities. The Book of Paul's Epistles (or letters) in the New Testament is an example of the kind of support and encouragement sent through these early mail systems. Eventually, Christianity would become accepted, and would become a major power within the Roman Empire—and would lose some of its worldwide impact as the Roman Empire began to decline.

The Decline of Rome

Gradually, the center of power in the Roman Empire shifted eastward. In the empire's early days, emperors came from Rome or from the western provinces. But from the third century on, many were drawn from Illyria (present-day Albania) or even farther east.

These eastern-born emperors made their headquarters in the east as well. They chose various eastern cities to live in—until the Emperor Constantine actually founded a "New Rome" at the city of Byzantium. The city later became known as Constantinople in his honor. (Today it is called Istanbul.)

In 313 A.D. Constantine made another momentous change: he legalized Christianity throughout the empire. At this point, Constantinople became Rome's equal in power. Both Christianity and the Roman Empire began to split into eastern and western halves.

New Peoples. At the same time, new peoples from even a farther east were threatening the easternmost boundary of the Roman

Empire. The Romans fought them off, using the Via Egnatia as a means for transporting their army. Some of the Gothic peoples, who had reached Byzantium/Constantinople about a century earlier, had by the fourth century taken most of the Balkans (parts of present-day Albania, Yugoslavia, Bulgaria, and Rumania), holding the Romans largely to the corridor around the Egnatian Way. The Goths threatened to break up the Via Egnatia, splitting Rome and Constantinople apart.

By the beginning of the fifth century, the Goths were using the empire's roads against the empire itself. They marched along the Egnatian Way into Macedonia and Greece.

The Visigoths took another convenient Roman road up the Illyrian coast, around the Adriatic Sea and into Italy. There they shocked the world by sacking Rome. (The western Roman government had left the city to them, retreating farther south.) The Goths took whatever valuables they wanted from Rome and moved west, in whole communities at a time, driving herds of cattle and riding in covered wagons.

Ironically, the Goths admired the Romans so much that they actually rebuilt and repaired part of the Appian Way, trying to imitate the famous Romans. The Romans, in turn, tried to make the Goths a part of the Roman Empire, as they had done with so many other peoples. But new peoples continued to move into Italy, which in the coming centuries gradually split into many different, tiny states. The Appian Way was no longer controlled by a single power.

Two Empires. The Appian and the Egnatian Ways pulled apart, no longer joining a single, united empire. The eastern half of the old empire became known as the *Byzantine Empire*.

Of course, the main road in this new empire was the Egnatian Way. Unlike the Via Appia, the Egnatian Way kept its importance for some time. For a while it was the Byzantine Empire's main connection between its capital, Constantinople, and the western territories.

Then the Avars swept into the Balkans from what is now Hungary. The Byzantine rulers called for help from the Serbs and the Croats. After the Avars were driven back into Hungary, the Serbs and Croats stayed in the empire, moving through the Balkans, where they still live today. At about the same time, the Bulgars (residents of today's Bulgaria) also arrived. Soon after, the Wallachs, or Vlachs, followed.

All these peoples settled along the Egnatian Way. Eventually, they cut off the land connections between Rome and Constantinople. For most of the seventh and eighth centuries, people had to travel by sea between east and west. In the ninth and 10th centuries, the Bulgar Empire settled along the Egnatian Way, so that this route began to be used once again.

EAST AGAINST WEST

In this period a split began to develop among the peoples along the Egnatian Way that would have great impact in the world. The newer immigrants along the route became Christians—but Christians who were split between East and West. From Bulgaria eastwards, Christians followed the rule of the emperor in Constantinople. West of Bulgaria, Christians were led by the pope in Rome. Romans spoke Latin: citizens of Constantinople spoke Greek.

Over the centuries, other differences developed between the two groups. Each had different customs, which included different practices in shaving hair, eating meat, eating unleavened bread, and counting the days of the fasting period known as Lent. Religious interpretations differed, too. Eventually, there was a great split, or *schism*, between the Eastern church (Greek Orthodox) and the Western Church (Catholic; later called "Roman" Catholic).

THE CRUSADES

Ironically, though the eastern and western branches of Christianity opposed each other, they joined together to oppose a third group—the Turks.

Over the centuries, pilgrims had been allowed to visit Christian shrines in Moslem territory, passing eastward on the Egnatian Way to do so. But the Turks had recently converted to Islam and their power was growing in the eastern empire. They decided to keep the Christians out of their territory. They attacked Constantinople and closed the pilgrimage routes. The Byzantine emperor appealed to the Catholic Pope for aid. Together, they launched the First Crusade.

The Crusades were launched in the name of reconquering land that the Christian religion considered holy—regions in the Middle East that include present-day Israel. Besides religious motives,

In the 17th century, as today, travelers on the Appian Way followed the old Roman cut around the hill of Terracina. (Engraving by Braun, Florence; Autostrade S.P.A.)

people who went on the Crusades had political and economic motives as well. Nobles hoped to capture land and loot, while cities in Italy wanted to reestablish trade with the East. There were several crusades from the 11th through the 13th centuries. In each, the Appian or the Egnatian Ways were used for transportation.

Roads and the Crusades. At first, the Appian Way was one of the main routes used by Italian crusaders. From the Appian, they crossed the Adriatic Sea, joined others who had come down the Illyrian coast, and took the Egnatian Way to Constantinople.

One group of Normans, a people from northern France, did not follow the route to its end, but ignored the Turks and went back to attack Illyria, then part of Byzantine territory. The Byzantines were furious that their western allies had attacked them instead of their common enemy. They fought the Normans and defeated them, but much of the western part of the Egnatian Way was destroyed in the process.

Pilgrims. Eventually, the Crusades ended, with no real gain in territory for the Christian countries. Meanwhile, the Via Appia was seeing Christian activity of another kind. Hundreds of thousands of pilgrims were coming to Rome, the center of their religion.

These pilgrimages were especially popular around the end of the 16th and the beginning of the 17th centuries. Pilgrims traveling on the Appian Way noted the old Roman ruins, sadly describing the remains of the once beautiful villas and palaces. Soon the ruins were destroyed: throughout the Middle Ages and the Renaissance, the Italians raided the Via Appia and its monuments for building materials. The ancient Italian church that you visit today may be built of stones taken from monuments along the Appian Way—or from the stones of the road itself.

THE TURKS

Just as the Appian Way tells the story of the West, the Egnatian Way tells the story of the East. Although the Byzantines had defeated the Normans who attacked them during the Crusades, they were weakened by the battles. When the Serbs began a drive for power along the Egnatian Way, the Byzantines had to call in the Turks to help drive them out.

The Turks did drive out the Serbs—but then they themselves stayed.

From the middle of the 13th century, more and more Turks moved along the Egnatian Way, often driving local settlers up into the hills or across the Adriatic into Italy. In 1453, the Turks took Constantinople, the city that even today, as Istanbul, is part of modern Turkey. Although the Turks drove out the Italians from much of this area, they were not able to maintain the huge empire that had conquered so many lands centuries ago.

Other immigrants traveled east in the Middle Ages. Jewish refugees, thrown out of Spain and Portugal, settled in the area. Yet without an empire controlled by a single power, it was difficult to maintain the old roads that linked together the territories. The Turks repaired only the parts of the Egnatian Way that they found most useful, letting the rest decline until, by the 16th century, trees grew in the middle of some parts of the road. Travelers made detours around such barriers, bringing bends and curves into the once-straight Roman road.

Modern Times: New Powers in Europe

By the 19th century, there were new empires fighting for world power. The old Roman and Byzantine influence could still be felt in the languages, cultures, and religions of Europe and the Middle East. But actual political power was held by other European nations.

A turning point in world history came with the defeat of Napoleon, the French emperor who had conquered many European territories, including much of Italy. If he was superior on land, he still had to face the mighty British navy, which blockaded him at sea. Once again, the Appian Way became important: It connected Rome with Naples, a key supply port. During the blockade, important supplies from the south could be taken north by land.

The British defeated Napoleon, however, in 1815, thus becoming the major force in the Mediterranean. Although Italy always remained politically independent of Britain, many British tourists were interested in Italy, and were fascinated by the Roman ruins of the past. With such interest, the Appian Way revived.

An eruption of Mt. Vesuvius in the 17th century disturbed travel on the Naples spur of the Appian Way, as an earlier eruption had destroyed the city of Pompeii. (From Jean Blaeu, *Nouveau Thèâtre d'Italie,* 1704)

Meanwhile, the Egnatian Way fell into disuse. By 1912, Turkish lands had been trimmed to the corridor around the Way, just as Roman lands had been cut back in the fourth century A.D. The beginning of World War I—provoked by a Serbian assassin in the Austrian province of Bosnia—brought world powers even more directly into the region and the Turks withdrew further.

After World War I, the territory around the Egnatian Way was redivided. Albania kept the mountain country at the western end of the route, Turkey was cut back to the Hebros River, and Greece was left with the coastal strip in between.

At this time, Greece and Turkey, longtime enemies, once again fought a war. Afterwards, when the borders were redrawn, many ethnic Greeks left the homes where they had lived for centuries in order to get out of Turkey. Likewise, many Turks left their long-time homes along the Egnatian Way. The Greeks and Turks each went to territories controlled by people of their own nationality.

Fascism in Italy. In the 1920s, Italy came under the rule of Benito Mussolini, a fascist dictator who dreamed of reviving the old Roman Empire and making Italy a world power once again. He too sent his armies southward and eastward, across the Adriatic to Albania during World War II.

Italy's ally, Germany, later passed through the region, traveling southward into Greece. The fascist German government had a policy of seeking out, imprisoning, and murdering Jews in any country in which they lived. Most of the large Jewish population of the Greek city, Thessalonica, was murdered or sent to concentration (prison) camps at this time.

After World War II ended, civil war broke out in Greece. Forces supported by powers in the west battled with Greeks who wanted communism to be the political ideology of their country. The final battle between the two groups was fought in a central passageway along the Egnatian Way. The communists were defeated, and the borders along the Egnatian Way settled into their present-day lines.

The Roads Today. Today, a traveler would find it almost impossible to travel from one end of the old Egnatian Way to another. Asphalt roads and railroads do cross the region, but political borders have changed the shape of the area. Albania allows very few foreigners to cross its borders.

The Via Appia, remaining within a single country, has been modified so that it has become a modern road. Some traffic still

In recent centuries, travelers have found largely ruins—fallen or pulled down—along the Appian Way. (By Jakob Wilhelm Mechau, Goethe-Museum, Düsseldorf)

travels on the old two-lane Appia, now part of Statale (State Road) 17. At the city of Brindisi, travelers can still see the two columns that marked the end of the Via Appia. Many maps still mark the road "Via Appia Antica." And even if many Italians do now know who Appius Claudius was, his road is surely remembered every day. Ask for directions south from Rome, and you will be told, "Take the Appia ..."

SUGGESTIONS FOR FURTHER READING

Charlesworth, Martin Percival. *Trade-Routes and Commerce of the Roman Empire* (London: Cambridge University Press, 1924).

Chevallier, Raymond. *Roman Roads* (Berkeley and Los Angeles: University of California Press, 1976), translated from the French by N. H. Field.

Hamblin, Dora Jane and Mary Jane Grunsfeld. *The Appian Way: A Journey* (New York: Random House, 1974). Explores various aspects of the route, with notes on remains to be seen and some fine black-and-white photographs.

Leighton, Albert C. *Transport and Communication in Early Medieval Europe, A.D. 500–1100* (Newton Abbot, Devonshire: David Charles, 1972).

O'Sullivan, Firmin. *The Egnatian Way* (Harrisburg, Pa.: Stackpole Books, 1972).

Rose, Albert Chatellier. "*Via Appia* in the Days When All Roads Led to Rome," *Smithsonian Report for 1934*, pp. 347-70. A useful summary, focusing on construction methods for the Appian Way and other Roman roads.

Rostovtzeff, M. *The Social and Economic History of the Roman Empire*, two vols., second edition, revised by P. M. Fraser (Oxford: Clarendon Press, 1957).

Sitwell, N. H. H. *Roman Roads of Europe* (New York: St Martin's, 1981).

Skeel, Caroline A. J. *Travel in the First Century After Christ: With Special Reference to Asia Minor* (Cambridge: at the University Press, 1901).

Von Hagen, Victor Wolfgang. *The Roads That Led to Rome* (Cleveland: World, 1967).

3

THE GREAT NORTH ROAD

THE ROMANCE OF THE ROAD

The wind was a torrent of darkness among the gusty trees,
The moon was a ghostly galleon tossed upon cloudy seas,
The road was a ribbon of moonlight over the purple moor,
And the highwayman came riding—Riding—riding—
The highwayman came riding, up to the old inn-door.

—From "The Highwayman" by Alfred Noyes

The highwayman is gone now. Indeed, he had been gone for more than half a century when Alfred Noyes wrote about him in 1906. By then, the great stagecoach post roads of England, Scotland, Wales, and Cornwall had long since been overtaken by the railroad. Soon the railroad would be overtaken by asphalt highways and speeding automobiles. But the air of romance still clings to those old English roads: the outlaw highwayman, riding over the dark moors with only the moon to guide him; the old inn, with its local farmers gathered comfortably around a blazing fire, drinking ale and swapping stories; and perhaps a mysterious lady fleeing a mysterious danger…

The real story of England's roads may not be quite so romantic! But it is true that these roads have fascinated writers and storytellers almost since the Romans first built them 2,000 years ago. And it is also true that the story of these roads is in many ways the story of England.

The Great North Road

——————	Main Roman North Road (Ermine Street)	-------	Roman Akeman Street
——————	Route Uncertain	— — —	Fosse Way
—··—··—	Modern Great North Road	··········	Main Connecting Roads
—-----	Roman Watling Street	—··—··—	Hadrian's Wall
		-------	Antonine Wall

The Great North Road. The greatest of England's roads was called Ermine Street in Roman times. Later it was known as the Old North Road. Since coaching days, it has been known as the Great North Road. From the river city of London, this highway pushes north across the wet clay of the Midlands, through the Yorkshire Moors, and into Scotland's capital, Edinburgh.

Great Britain and Its Kingdoms. Some people get confused about names when studying Britain. Many people confuse "Britain" with "England." In fact, "Britain" is the name for the entire island, only a part of which is England. Also on that island are the countries of Scotland and Wales. These areas were for many years politically independent, with their own language and culture.

The term "Great Britain" includes the part of Ireland, known as Northern Ireland, that Britain retains control of today. The Irish were also a separate nation with their own language and culture. Today there is a part of Ireland that is politically separate from Great Britain and a part of Ireland that belongs to Great Britain.

For England to grow into Great Britain, it needed a road to unite it and to reach the territories it conquered. That road was eventually to be called the Great North Road.

ROMAN ROADS

Before the Romans. Little is known of the early, Bronze Age peoples of Britain. We do know about Stonehenge, a circle of huge, standing stones that was probably used in some kind of religious ceremony. This amazing monument suggests that the peoples of England had a complicated and highly developed culture.

In the fifth century B.C., Britain was invaded by the Celtic people. After many centuries had passed, the Celts were restricted to the part of Britain that is now Ireland.

We know much more about what happened to Britain after 55 B.C. In that year, the Roman military leader Julius Caesar landed at Dover in the southeast of England with two Roman legions. Caesar was trying to conquer new lands for the Roman Empire, a huge world power. We know more about this time because the Romans kept written records.

The Romans, at their empire's height, controlled territories in the modern countries of France, Italy, Spain, Turkey, Greece, Albania, and Yugoslavia, as well as territories in the Middle East region. They were somewhat less interested in Britain than in other parts of Europe, because they had to cross the sea to reach Britain. Also, at the time Caesar first entered Britain, the Romans were not as strong as they were later to become. Thus Caesar visited Britain twice in two years, but did not stay or leave soldiers behind him to keep control of the territory.

In the summer of 43 A.D., the Roman Emperor Claudius carried out another invasion of Britain. This time, he drew soldiers and supplies from a very great empire, for Rome had been controlling much of Western Europe for over a hundred years. Claudius's base was the city of Lyon, in Gaul (modern-day France), across the sea from Britain. There Claudius held camels and elephants in reserve to use against the Britons.

The Romans landed in Britain at several points along the coast. At this time, they had more advanced weapons and military techniques than the natives of Britain, so they were able to dominate the local peoples, who lived in isolated villages and small towns.

Roman troops moved through the country following old local pathways, sometimes carving new routes. One of the skills they had developed was the building of roads, which they then used both for military purposes—so that soldiers and troop supplies could move easily—and for trade and other travel. They used these road-building skills to conquer England, and to hold it for another three and a half centuries.

You can imagine what an advantage these roads gave the Romans. They could move their troops easily through the many small kingdoms, send messages back and forth by special couriers, and make sure that all troops were fed and clothed with supplies from across the country. One main road, Fosse Way, was not just a road but also a long, fortified wall, which divided the conquered parts of Britain from the unconquered parts. The fortifications were good protection against attack.

Aerial photographs still show the old line of the Roman Ermine Street, running straight across the field, while the more modern Great North Road curves in from the right near Stamford. (British Air Ministry)

Ermine Street. The Romans also began a new road, called Ermine Street, the beginning of what would later be called the Great North Road. Ermine Street became their main military highway as they completed their British conquests. After conquering the southern part of Britain, they kept pushing farther north, all the way into what is now Scotland.

The Fighting Caledonians. The people of that area were called Caledonians, ancestors of today's Scots. They fought the Romans in the Scottish Highlands in 83 A.D. The Roman invaders won the battle at Mons Graupius, but did not follow up and never occupied the entire island. For centuries afterwards, the northern peoples resisted Roman rule. The Roman writer Tacitus quotes a battlefield speech made by Calgacus, the leader of the Caledonians. Calgacus spoke movingly about how much the Caledonians hated the tyranny of Rome:

> We, the choicest flowers of Britain ... kept even our eyes free from the defilement of tyranny. We, the last men on earth, the last of the free, have been shielded until today by the very remoteness and the seclusion for which we are famed ... But today the boundary of Britain is exposed; beyond us lies no nation, nothing but waves and rocks and the Romans...

The Romans like to say that they brought "Pax Romana"—the Roman peace—to the areas that they conquered. Calgacus had another opinion. He said, "They create a desolation, and call it peace."

Because of the northern resistance, the northern part of Ermine Street was mainly a military road, with war chariots a more common form of traffic than farmers' carts. In any case, Rome did not hold the north country for very long. In 142 A.D., the army built the 37-mile-long Antonine Wall to mark the boundary between them and the Caledonians who were still free. Later they had to pull back even farther, to the 71-mile-long wall named after the Emperor Hadrian. For centuries, Hadrian's Wall would be the northern border of Roman Britain—and the end of the Great North Road.

THE DECLINE OF ROME

The Roman Empire held England and part of Scotland for almost 400 years, but by the late fourth century A.D., Roman power was weakening. At this point, invaders from many different places were attacking the Roman Empire's European territories. Rome could no longer spare so many troops and supplies to keep Britain under its control. It needed them for its own defense.

By the fifth century, no more troops and supplies at all came from Rome. By the end of the century, Roman rule in Britain had fallen apart.

The conquering Romans had held the different peoples and regions of England and Scotland together, keeping up the roads that made communication possible. When Roman rule ended, the country broke up into many smaller kingdoms. This process was accelerated by the many different invasions of Britain from people of many different lands. Many of these invaders became the ancestors of today's Britons, leaving their own mark on the country's culture and language.

Picts and Scots. Beginning in 367 A.D., Pictish raiders came down from the north over Hadrian's Wall. The Picts were ancient inhabitants of northern and central Scotland. Many centuries later, in 843 A.D., they joined with the Scottish kingdom of Dalriada to form the kingdom of Scotland.

Anglo-Saxons. The Anglo-Saxons spoke Germanic languages; that is, languages that came from the area that is now the country of Germany. They were actually composed of three different peoples, the Angles, the Saxons, and the Jutes, each of whom settled in a different part of England.

Celts. The Celts are the ancestors of the modern-day Irish. They, too, came from Germany, but they had moved all over Europe by the fifth and sixth centuries B.C. In Britain, the Celtic language was spoken in Ireland, the Scottish Hebrides and Highlands, Wales, and Cornwall. In France, the Celtic language was spoken in Brittany. Today, these names all refer to countries or regions, either in Great Britain or in France, but in the first centuries A.D., these names were the names of kingdoms.

Danes. The Danes invaded England in the eighth and ninth centuries. By 1016 A.D. King Canute, perhaps the most famous Viking, ruled all of England.

Many People, Many Kingdoms. Without a single military power maintaining the Great North Road, the road tended to fall into disrepair. However, it was still used by the many peoples of England and Scotland as the road passed through many different little kingdoms. A late-ninth-century map shows the Great North Road passing through a number of different regions, including Wessex, East Anglia, Danish Mercia, York, Northumberland, and Scotland. These areas in turn were cut up into smaller counties and provinces ruled by various feudal lords and aristocrats.

THE NORMAN CONQUEST

Then, in the year 1066, came an event that was to change the entire course of European history—the Norman Conquest. The Normans were a Viking people living in Normandy, in northwest France. The name *Norman* comes from *Norsemen*, people from Scandinavia.

The Norman Duke William became *William the Conqueror* after his triumph over King Harold of England. William went on to kill most of the Anglo-Saxon nobles, or to deprive them of their land, so that Norman aristocrats ruled over both Anglo-Saxon and Celtic peoples.

In addition, the Normans' version of French was spoken at court. This had an enormous impact on the present-day English language, which is derived from Anglo-Saxon Germanic languages. This "layering" effect of different types of languages on top of each other makes the English language very rich in vocabulary.

THE HIGH ROAD TO SCOTLAND

With the Norman Conquest, the outlines of what would become modern England began to be clear. Like the Roman invaders before him, William wanted to unify England under his own power. He had reasons to develop the high road north to Scotland: he needed both military control and increased trade.

In the 11th and 12th centuries, this trade often took the form of *fairs*, central marketplaces where traders could come together to buy and sell. English farmers drove their cattle to these fairs, hoping to get the best price for their livestock. Stourbridge, St. Ives, Winchester, and other so-called *market towns* flourished from these fairs. And a web of "green roads" were beaten down in the fields from town to town.

Like their earlier counterparts, these farmers are selling horses at a crossroads—a surefire place to find buyers. (By W.H. Pyne, from his *Picturesque Views of Rural Occupations in Early Nineteenth-Century England*)

CHRISTIAN PILGRIMS

The development of Christianity in England was a slow and uneven process. Picts, Celts, and Anglo-Saxons all had their own religions. Not until the mass Saxon conversions to Christianity in the seventh and eighth centuries was Christianity a real force in England, and even then it had to contend with the country's other religions for some time.

Those people who did become Christians often made pilgrimages to the sites they considered holy. By the late medieval times of the 14th and 15th centuries, the roads were full of religious travelers.

Pilgrims of Different Types. Some pilgrims were traveling to fulfill a vow. If they or their family had been sick and were now well, they might be repaying a promise to God to make a pilgrimage of thanks if the sick person recovered. Someone who believed he or she had sinned greatly might try to pay for or *atone* for the sin by making a pilgrimage.

At this time, most Christians in Western Europe were Catholics, who confessed their sins to priests. Sometimes a priest would order someone to atone for their sins with a pilgrimage. If the sin seemed especially terrible, the priest might order the traveler to go barefoot, or to wear only a thin shirt.

Parts of the Great North Road were dotted with shrines, roadside places of worship set up by the pilgrims. Pilgrims who were going to the mainland of Europe also took the Great North Road on their way South to the holy cities of Rome, Jerusalem, or Santiago de Compostela in Spain.

TRAVELERS, TRADERS, AND OUTLAWS

Can you imagine all the different types of people who might be traveling on the Great North Road during the medieval centuries? An innkeeper going to get supplies for his roadside business, so that he can sell food to other weary travelers. A wandering minstrel playing his instrument and singing his long story-songs, picking up money for his performances from travelers or townspeople. Jugglers and tumblers performing for travelers or people in the towns, picking up a few coins here and there.

Herbalists also traveled on the roads, selling remedies for all sorts of diseases, while fake doctors promised miracle cures to any who would believe them. Hurrying messengers knocked other travelers out of the way as they rode from post to post, carrying important messages from a lord to his ally in another part of England.

Meanwhile, peddlers plied their wares to the poor folk along the route, and merchants carried rich stores of silks or jewels or furs from Europe or the East. Wandering men searched for work along the road while free peasants looked for a farmer to hire them for a harvest season. A traveling preacher would plan a sermon for the next town, where he hoped to take up a large collection for his trouble; and a friar might move slowly on his way to a new monastery.

Outlaws. All of these travelers, however, feared outlaws, or *highwaymen*, men who hid along the highway to rob unsuspecting travelers of their money and goods. Highwaymen made the roads unsafe until the early 19th century. Poor and desperate, these men were very different from the romantic figure portrayed in Noyes's poem. They were often men who had been blacklisted by farmers, workshop owners, or other employers, so that they could not get any other kind of work.

There have traditionally been two ways of looking at highwaymen in England. On the one hand, they were feared by travelers who knew that an ambush by a desperate robber in a lonely place could cost them their lives. On the other hand, they were seen as romantic heroes, like Robin Hood, the outlawed noble who "stole from the rich to give to the poor." Perhaps some people in England sympathized with the reasons that might have turned a highwayman to crime, even though they were also sometimes scared to travel.

Different Means of Transportation

Until the mid-1500s, most long-distance travel on the Great North Road and other main roads was on horseback, with baggage and trading goods carried by mule packtrains.

Drovers like this one—driving sheep, oxen, cattle, and other farm animals to market—marked out roads leading to and alongside the Great North Road. (By W.H. Pyne, from his *Picturesque Views of Rural Occupations in Early Nineteenth-Century England*)

Some people traveled on foot, especially farmers who drove their cattle along the wide green paths on either side of the road. In later years, when the roads became hard-surfaced, cattle used to cut their hooves on the gravel by the side of the roads. In those times, cattle blacksmiths along the Great North Road did a good trade in cattle-shoeing.

Carts and Carriages. Since before the Romans came, England's roads had been traveled by carts, and carts continued to roll for centuries afterward. But most carts were so heavy that they could travel only over hard ground. The soft clay of the Midlands and the boggy section north of London did not make good roads for carts.

Sometimes people tried to improve the roads by pouring gravel and dirt into the boggy areas. One traveler said that the bog just north of London had "swallowed up at least 20,000 cartloads" of fill.

By the early 1600s, carriages and heavier transport wagons had begun to travel on the Great North Road. These heavier vehicles required still greater road maintenance, which was expensive and difficult.

During this period, Queen Elizabeth enjoyed traveling throughout her kingdom in an open carriage, accompanied by hundreds of nobles, officials, and servants, plus many hundreds of baggage cars and wagons. Thousands of horses were needed to draw all these vehicles. Of course, this traffic also took its toll on the roads!

By the early 17th century, heavy four-wheeled wagons drawn by as many as 10 horses began to appear. They tore up the road so badly that in 1616, local justices put a five-horse limit on wagons. At about this time they also imposed strict weight limits on loads, hoping to protect the roads.

Despite these restrictions, road use continued to increase on the Great North Road. The 1640s saw the beginning of long-distance stagecoach runs, and the appearance of roadside inns to put coach travelers up for the night. Imagine the difference it would make in your decision to travel if you knew you could ride in a coach instead of on horseback, and if you knew you could have a comfortable place to stay for the night.

Great North Road Inns. These comforts were especially appreciated by the English and Scottish nobility, who traveled back and forth between England's capital of London and Scotland's capital of Edinburgh on the Great North Road. Today, England and

Inns like the Angel at Grantham (left) and the George at Stamford (right) have stood throughout much of the history of the Great North Road. (By Herbert Railton and Hugh Thomson, from W. Outram Tristram, *Coaching Days and Coaching Ways*, 1888)

This 18th-century British highwayman is the very picture of a gentleman-robber. (From Stanley Appelbaum, *Advertising Woodcuts from the Nineteenth-century Stage*, Dover, 1977)

Scotland are part of the same nation, the United Kingdom, but in those days they were two separate kingdoms, each with its own royal family. Many modern-day innkeepers along the road can tell you about the royalty that stayed in their inns so many years ago.

These inns were very popular with nobles, royalty and all sorts of other travelers. As the writer W. Outram Tristram described it:

All were here, we may be well assured ... all and of every rank, in a motley assemblage of confused travel—kings, queens, statesmen, highwaymen, generals, poets, wits, fine ladies, conspirators, and coachmen. [Over the centuries, they all] ate and drank, and robbed, or were robbed, and died, and made merry ...

In 1603, the thrones of England and Scotland were joined, and in 1707 the two countries were officially united to form a single nation. The Great North Road, which connected them, became even more important.

Snow and mud alike posed hazards to coaches; here the precious mail is being sent on ahead by a mounted courier, while help is being summoned. (After James Pollard, 1825, authors' archives)

The road was especially important to England because so many of the Scots were resistant to English dominance. The English-Scottish wars lasted until 1745, frequently requiring English troops to be sent north along the road. Of course, the very fighting that led England to send troops also made the sending of them more difficult. The roads were damaged in the fighting and were certainly not well repaired. After the English crushed the last great Scottish rising, they hired workers to rebuild and maintain the roads.

Postal Services. The Great North Road was also the main post road north, from London's General Post Office to that of Edinburgh. Postal services were more important than ever as businesses and political activities expanded to cover ever wider ranges. It was important for traders, merchants, and government officials to communicate quickly with people in other parts of the country.

The Great North Road was also the royal road, used by members of the royal family. And it was the road used most often by coaches

Heavily loaded freight wagons, like this one in 19th-century Northamptonshire, carved up the dirt roads in the years before the turnpike system. (After G. S. Shepherd, 1836, authors' archives)

traveling between north and south. Even so, the Great North Road was in terrible condition. How could a constant maintenance of the road be kept up to make travel easier and more comfortable?

Toll Roads and Turnpikes. The solution that the English came up with was to make travelers pay to use the road. Thus this road (and others) became known as a *toll road*, or *turnpike*, because to use it, you had to pay a toll, or fee.

The Great North Road was the first toll road, declared so by an Act of Parliament in 1633. The system was greatly disliked: people thought they should be able to travel for free, and traders complained that it made their business more expensive. Throughout England in the 18th century, travelers broke down toll gates, sometimes even burned them, and abused toll-gate keepers. But whether or not the toll system was liked, the roads did improve during this time.

GREAT COACHING DAYS

As the roads improved, especially in the late 18th and early 19th centuries, travel on the Great North Road grew greatly. Mail was now carried by coach, rather than by messenger—and in the coaches, passengers could ride.

Increased coach travel brought more and bigger inns along the roads. By the end of the 18th century, dozens of mail coaches left London each day. Each carried the mail, four to six inside passengers, and a driver and an armed guard on top. The greater amount of travel began to discourage highwaymen, as did stronger policing along the road.

Coach travel was really popular for only about 50 years, from the end of the 18th century to early in the 19th century—just until the growth of railroads. However, this short period was remembered very romantically. Travel by coach was highly praised by contemporary writer Charles Dickens, who described the pleasures of traveling the high roads in his novel, *The Pickwick Papers*:

> They have rumbled through the streets, and jolted over the stones, and at length reach the wide and open country. The wheels skim over the hard and frosty ground; and the horses, bursting into a canter at a smart crack of the whip, step along the road as if the load behind them—coach, passengers, codfish and oyster-barrels, and all—were but a feather at their heels. They have descended a gentle slope, and enter upon a level, as compact and dry as a solid block of marble, two miles long. Another crack of the whip, and on they speed at a smart gallop, the horses tossing

Unhappiness over the toll system led to complaints and fights for many years; here a stagecoach awaits the outcome of a fight before passing through the gate. (By Herbert Railton and Hugh Thomson, from W. Outram Tristram, *Coaching Days and Coaching Ways*, 1888)

After each stop, the stagecoach would set off again with a great bustle; here the footman brandishes his horn in a farewell wave. (By Herbert Railton and Hugh Thomson, from W. Outram Tristram, *Coaching Days and Coaching Ways*, 1888)

their heads and rattling the harness, as if in exhilaration at the rapidity of the motion; while the coachman, holding whip and reins in one hand, takes off his hat with the other, and resting it on his knees, pulls out his handkerchief, and wipes his forehead, partly because he has a habit of doing it, and partly because it's as well to show the passengers how cool he is, and what an easy thing it is to drive four-in-hand when you have had as much practice as he has. Having done this very leisurely (otherwise the effect would be materially impaired), he replaces his handkerchief, pulls on his hat, adjusts his gloves, squares his elbows, cracks the whip again, and on they speed, more merrily than before ...

And now the bugle plays a lively air as the coach rattles through the ill-paved streets of a country town; and the coachman, undoing the buckle which keeps his ribands together, prepares to throw them off the moment he stops.

He throws down the reins and gets down himself, and the other outside passengers drop down also; except those who have no great confidence in their ability to get up again; and they remain where they are, and stamp their feet against the coach to warm them—looking, with longing eyes and red noses, at the bright fire in the inn bar, and the sprigs of holly with red berries which ornament the window ... [Then] the coachman shouts an admonitory "Now then, gen'l'm'n" the guard reechoes it; the old gentleman inside thinks it a very extraordinary thing that people *will* get down when they know there isn't time for it; shawls are pulled up, coat collars are readjusted, the pavement ceases, the houses disappear; and they are once again dashing along the open road, with the fresh air flowing in their faces, and gladdening their very hearts within them.

ROAD IMPROVEMENTS

All through the coaching days, the roads continued to improve. Thomas Telford built roads with a firm foundation of large rocks, covering that foundation with a six-inch layer of broken rocks. Then he laid gravel on top of that. That strong construction could support many thousands of pounds of horse and carriage travel. Telford also made sure to curve his roads' surfaces, so that water would drain off to the side. That way, people could travel his roads even in rainy or snowy weather..

John McAdam invented a new method of building roads in the 19th century that was named after him: he used a thin surface of broken rocks bound together by stone chips and dust. In modern times, we call *macadam* roads after John McAdam.

RAILWAYS AND HIGHWAYS

In 1838, the year after Dickens described coaching in *The Pickwick Papers*, the mails began to go by rail instead of by road. This was the beginning of the end of coaching days, and the beginning of a drastic change in the importance of the Great North Road.

The railroads grew rapidly. By 1850, over 6,000 miles of track had been opened in Britain, and the coaches had all but disappeared. You may still see old coach timetables on the walks of old inns.

After the railroads came the highways. Britain's multi-lane highway, the A1, generally follows the route of the Great North Road—but not exactly. Instead of passing through the centers of cities and towns, it bypasses them to allow greater speed.

Still, if you travel north from London to Edinburgh today, you can find bits of the Great North Road, old inns from the past century or two, and at some points you will even be following the course of the old Roman road exactly. The legacy of the Great North Road remains a living presence in the midst of modern times.

Suggestions for Further Reading

Addison, William. *The Old Roads of England* (London: Batsford, 1980).

Cottrell, Leonard. *A Guide to Roman Britain* (Wilkes-Barre, Pennsylvania: Dimension, 1966).

Harper, Charles G. *The Great North Road: The Old Mail Road to Scotland*, vol. 1: London to York; vol. 2: York to Edinburgh (London: Chapman & Hall, 1901).

Hindley, Geoffrey. *A History of Roads* (Secaucus, N.J.: Citadel, 1972).

Jusserand, J. J. *English Wayfaring Life in the Middle Ages* (New York: Putnam, 1889).

Morely, Frank. *The Great North Road* (New York: Macmillan, 1961).

Sitwell, N. H. H. *Roman Roads of Europe* (New York: St. Martins, 1981).

Trevelyan, G. M. *English Social History* (London: Longmans, 1942).

Tristram, W. Outram. *Coaching Days and Coaching Ways* (London: Macmillan, 1888).

Von Hagen, Victor W. *The Roads that Led to Rome* (World: Cleveland, 1967).

Walbank, F. Alan, ed. *The English Scene* (New York: Scribner, 1946).

Wood, Anthony. *Nineteenth Century Britain* (London: Longmans, 1960).

4

THE HERACLEAN WAY

THE TRAVELS OF HERCULES

The Greeks called him "Heracles." The Romans called him "Hercules." But both agreed: he was the strongest human being in the world. Both Greek and Roman myths also say that Hercules' travels took him throughout much of Europe and Asia and that, wherever he went, he accomplished heroic deeds that defy imagination.

When Hercules traveled through the huge, snowy mountains known as the Alps, he was supposed to have cleared paths for future travelers, heaving enormous boulders out of the way, smoothing roads, and killing the robber chiefs that had menaced other travelers. When he traveled by ship with another mythical hero, Jason, he helped Jason to win the Golden Fleece.

But the most famous of Hercules' travels were along the coast road between Italy and the Atlantic coast of Spain. As the story goes, this is the route along which he traveled when he performed his legendary 12 labors, the superhuman tasks he undertook to do penance for a terrible deed he had committed.

Hercules moved through Italy to Gaul, or modern France. There, he supposedly put down the practice of human sacrifice and conquered the area that today is the rich vacation beachland known as the Riviera.

When Hercules reached his western goal of Iberia (now Spain and Portugal), he is supposed to have killed a monster ruling over the local people. The myth goes on to tell us that he pushed apart the continents of Europe and Africa, planting massive rocks on both sides of the strait between the Mediterranean Sea and the Atlantic Ocean. These rocks were the famous Pillars of Hercules: "Jebel

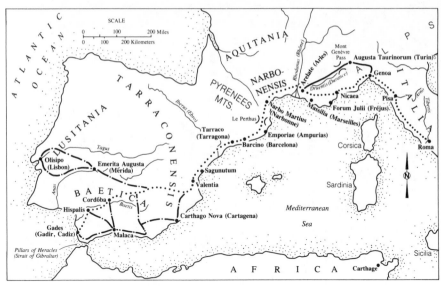

The Heraclean Way in Greek and Roman Times

········ The Heraclean Way   ———— Alternate Routes in Gaul

—·—·— Alternate Routes in Hispania

Musa" on the African side and "the Rock of Gibraltar" on the European side.

Hercules is only a mythical character. But many ancient leaders dreamed of following in his footsteps to win control of the whole area between Italy and the Atlantic Ocean. No one succeeded—until the Roman Empire took control of the area. When it did, the empire built its longest continuous route, stretching 1,700 miles from Rome to Gades (the modern city of Cadiz, Spain), on the coast of the Atlantic Ocean. It named this road the *Via Herculea*, or *Heraclean Way*, after the journey taken by the mythical hero, Hercules.

THE STORY OF THE HERACLEAN WAY

Looking at the history of the Heraclean Way is much like looking at the history of any other trade route. As we read about how this road was built and who used it, we are reading the history of the people and the use of power in that region.

In the case of the Heraclean Way, we are reading the story of a land that was continually conquered by those from outside. This area—coastal Italy, the French Riviera, Spain, and Portugal—was located very strategically between several different empires. Over the centuries, as different empires rose and fell, they sought to expand and take possession of this area. Not until modern times could this area have been said to rule itself.

Before the Conquerors Came

The early peoples along the route came from many different places. In about 2000 B.C., the area south of the Pyrenees Mountains (modern-day Spain) was populated by the Iberians. These people took their name from the river Iberus (today called Ebro).

Along the Italian coastal strip lived the Ligurians, Celtic people who had migrated south from Gaul and northern Italy. (Today these people live in a region of Italy called Liguria.)

The Italian peninsula was populated by people called the Italics. In about 1200 B.C. they were joined by the Etruscans, who settled between the Tiber and Arno Rivers.

During this period, the ancient land-track was primarily a local route, although sometimes people used it to make long-distance migrations. But regular trade and transportation along this route was rare, and did not really begin until peoples who lived in the eastern part of the Mediterranean pushed west to mine the valuable copper, tin and silver to be found. The first foreign peoples to come into this region only wanted to trade. Later some of these visitors would want to conquer, as well.

The Phoenicians

The first people to enter the western Mediterranean in any large numbers were the Phoenicians. They were a people who lived in a coastal area centered on today's Lebanon. By 1250 B.C., they were the most famous navigators and traders in the world. They eventually expanded their commercial boundaries to found the cities of Utica and Carthage (15 miles apart, near modern-day Tunis in North Africa). The Phoenicians were the people who invented the idea of the alphabet, an idea later adopted by the Greeks.

At some point after 1100 B.C., Phoenician traders made their way west, to the regions along the Heraclean Way. Passing through the Pillars of Hercules (the Strait of Gibraltar), they founded a settlement they called Gadir, which means enclosure, and which today is the city of Cadiz. Their port was on an easy-to-defend neck of land jutting out into the Atlantic Ocean, with a fine harbor. This became one of the main ports on the Heraclean Way.

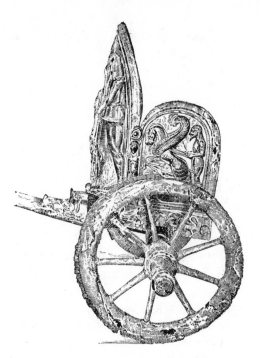

On the roads just north of Rome, the Etruscans sometimes used finely crafted chariots like this one made of bronze. (From James Henry Breasted, *Ancient Times: A History of The Early World …*, 1914)

The Phoenicians concentrated on southern Iberia. They were more interested in trading posts than in bases for conquest. But by the sixth century B.C., their homeland had fallen, conquered by the Persians. The Phoenician traders from Carthage then became more interested in Iberia—and Gadir (Cadiz) began to grow.

The Greeks

While the Carthaginians were focusing on southern Iberia, the Greeks concentrated on northern Iberia and Gaul. Their main base was at the city of Massilia (today called Marseilles). They also founded many other ports along the Heraclean Way, including the ancestors of modern-day Antibes and Nice, famous luxury resort towns along the French Riviera. The tiny country of Monaco, famous today for its gambling casinos and royal family , began as an early Phoenician site taken over by the Greeks, who called it Heracles Monacus (Hercules Living-Alone).

The Impact of the First Visitors

When trade and travel along the Heraclean Way began to increase, pack horses and wagons were used to carry tin and other precious goods. Yet the traders and travelers were not always safe. Sometimes they were asked by the local people to pay "tolls" for using the roads. These "tolls" were really "protection" money, the price travelers had to pay to make sure that local people would not attack or rob them. The tolls also paid for the assistance of local people at ferry crossings and portages (a portage is a dry place along a river journey where people must carry their boats and their baggage overland until they reach the water again).

THE RISE OF ROME

In about 500 B.C., the eastern part of the Heraclean Way was shared by the Ligurians and the Etruscans. In about 400 B.C., they were overrun by another group of Celts moving southward, this time over the Alps and into Italy. These Celts overcame the Etruscans and sacked the city of Rome, which was still very small.

But this tiny city of Rome was about to become the center of a huge empire spreading through all of Europe and parts of Asia, an empire that would control the land around the Heraclean Way.

The Roman Empire would shape the face of Europe. The empire itself gave the countries it had conquered a common language—Latin, the root language for modern Italian, Spanish, Portuguese, and French. Centuries later, when Christianity became the official Roman religion, the Catholic Church, based in Rome, became a major religious power in all the Roman lands, including Italy, Spain, Portugal, and France. Rome's culture would affect the lands around the Heraclean Way right up until our own day.

First Steps: The Latin League. The first step in the growth of Rome was the formation of the Latin League, an association of Italian cities organized to fight the Celts. After the cities jointly defeated the Celts, they began to dispute for power among themselves. Rome emerged as the strongest of the Latin League members.

The growing city had soon defeated all the peoples of Italy south of the Alps. The Romans also controlled the Greek coastal areas as far west as the river Iberus (Ebro) in Spain. Rome and Carthage now shared the western Mediterranean—and the Heraclean Way—between them.

Roman Roads. Unlike the seafaring peoples of the Mediterranean, the Romans were landlubbers. They used roads to conquer and hold

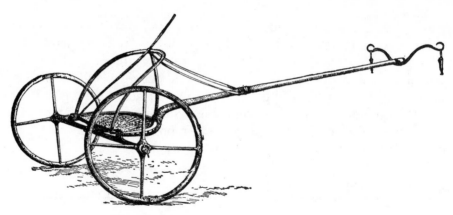

Chariots like this one, built of elm and ash and bound together with birch fiber, were used along the early Heraclean Way. (From James Henry Breasted, *Ancient Times: A History of The Early World ...,* 1914)

the territories of their empire. Roads were used by soldiers to march into new territory and to conquer it. Strong, solid, well-paved roads allowed horsedrawn and oxdrawn carts to carry food and supplies for the soldiers, making the Roman forces the strongest in the world.

After Rome had conquered a territory, it used roads to keep up its presence in the area. Roads made it easy for soldiers to enter an area, to put down an uprising or remind the people of Rome's military might. Roads were also used by swift couriers riding between the conquered territories and the capital city, carrying news of different parts of the empire and instructions on how the various areas were to be governed.

Last but not least, roads were used by the traders and traveling workers who tied the empire together by doing business in all its far-flung parts.

The first major Roman road was called the Via Appia, or Appian Way (see Chapter 2). The Via Appia ran south from Rome through the newly conquered peoples of Italy, cementing Rome's hold on its early conquests.

But the Romans built other roads soon after. In 241 B.C., construction began on the Via Aurelia, the first section of the Heraclean Way, beginning in Rome and reaching north up the Mediterranean coast. The construction was soon halted, however, when the Carthaginians began to attack the power of Rome.

HANNIBAL'S WAR

By this time, the Phoenician Empire had long since lost its power. But the city of Carthage, first developed by the Phoenicians, had emerged as a power of its own. While the Romans were beginning construction on the Heraclean Way, Carthage was beginning to develop its Iberian outposts into full-fledged colonies. Had the Carthaginians succeeded, the face of Europen culture might well be different today.

New Carthage. The Carthaginians began their expansion into Iberia slowly. They founded a major new port called Carthago Nova, which means New Carthage (it's now called Cartagena, in modern Spain). They also widened and improved the part of the Heraclean Way that crossed Iberia.

The Romans were suspicious of all this activity. They questioned the purpose of the road-building, but were assured that the Carthaginians were simply trying to move precious metals more efficiently. In fact, the Carthaginians, under their leader Hannibal, were planning to attack Rome, using the Heraclean Way.

Hannibal's Strategy. Hannibal was one of the greatest military geniuses of all time. He marched along the coast road, took the hilltop fort of Saguntum from the Romans, and then dug in for the winter. Hannibal's army included cavalry (soldiers on horseback), infantry (soldiers on foot), slingers (fighters equipped with slingshots that threw stones), and his famous North African elephants, which carried baggage and supplies.

In the spring of 218 B.C., Hannibal began to push northeastward along the coast, crossing the Iberian (Spanish) Pyrenees into Gaul (France) and heading for Italy. On his way, he got help from the Celts.

The Romans sent an army by ship up the Rhône River, planning to meet Hannibal. They were sure he would follow the Heraclean Way to the usual river crossing, walking right into their trap. But Hannibal's spies warned him of the Roman position. Hannibal moved his army farther north so that he could cross the river safely.

Hannibal bought up all the local rafts and boats for his river crossing. Suddenly, he found himself facing unfriendly Celtic tribes on the other side of the river. Again, he put off his crossing and moved even farther north. He managed to trick the Celts, cross the river and keep going.

Crossing the Rhône. Imagine what a difficult time Hannibal must have had. He had to get soldiers and baggage across a swift-flowing river (it was much easier to cross farther south, but the Romans were waiting). Worse, he had to get his elephants across!

He came up with a clever plan. He and his men built a pier out of several rafts tied together and sticking out over the water. They got the female elephants, who were easier to drive, out onto the rafts. The males instinctively went after the females.

Then Hannibal and his men cut the rafts loose and sent them floating across the river. Most of the elephants made it safely across, although some fell off their rafts and were drowned. Some Roman authors paint a colorful picture of the elephants walking across underwater, holding only their trunks up in the air to breathe, but this does not seem very likely.

Hannibal Crosses the Alps. While the Romans were still waiting down in the south, Hannibal went north, through the Alps, accompanied by his Celtic allies. Hannibal had paid bribes and made treaties in order to avoid fighting with other Celts, who lived in the Alps, but some of them attacked him anyway. However, the Celts had one habit that made trouble for themselves. After they had accomplished a brave deed, they liked to brag loudly about it, and thus often gave away their position. Then Hannibal's army could ambush or surprise them.

It took Hannibal only a little more than two weeks to cross the Alps and reach Italy. Here he had the advantage of surprise, for the Romans were still waiting for him down in southern Gaul! And none of the Romans were well enough acquainted with the Alpine passes to follow him immediately. For the next 15 years, the Carthaginians and the Celts were able to stay in Italy.

Rome Fights Back. While Hannibal had been able to enter Italy unopposed, circling around the Roman army, the Romans were about to play the same trick. Some Roman troops tried to catch up to Hannibal, but others sailed over to Iberia and then took the coast road to the Iberian capital of New Carthage. They cut Hannibal's food and military supply lines and pushed the Carthaginians out of Iberia.

Hannibal himself could not continue to fight in Italy while he was cut off from his supplies in Iberia. Eventually he and some parts of his army had to cross the sea back to North Africa.

Roads in Spain

If Carthage had continued to rule Iberia, the history, language, and culture of modern Spain might have been very different. Instead, what is now modern Spain came under Roman rule.

The long years of fighting had reminded the Romans once again of the importance of good roads. They moved quickly to build them on the Iberian peninsula (which they now renamed as *Hispania*). In 206 B.C., working from both ends, they began to build a typically solid Roman road from Gades (Roman for Gadir, which is modern Cadiz) to the Pyrenees. This 980-mile section of the Heraclean Way was finished almost 100 years later, in 120 B.C.. This section of the Heraclean Way was the principal road in Hispania for the next 600 years of Roman rule.

Roads in France

At the eastern end of the Heraclean Way, roadbuilding did not resume so quickly. Even after the Carthaginians had been expelled from Italy, their ships attacked Rome's coastal territory and the Greek territory under Roman protection. Taking advantage of the confusion, the Gauls (the new name for the Celts in the north) came south to attack.

The Greek colony of Massilia (present-day Marseilles, in the south of France) asked Rome for protection against the Gauls' attacks from the north. The Romans did help—but they took control of part of the coast in exchange. They used it to build a road that would pass through Gaul to connect Rome with Iberia and Hispania.

New Construction

Once the attacks from the Gauls were put down, roadbuilding began in earnest. Even though the road wasn't really finished in 46 B.C., it was so close to completion that Roman military leader Julius Caesar was able to boast of having taken an army from Rome to Spain without getting its feet wet. This was quite a boast, considering the number of rivers and streams the legions had to cross. (By this time, Julius Caesar had used his reputation as a military genius to become a Roman dictator, the most important political position in Rome.)

These Roman roads were much better engineered than the earlier roads. Instead of winding around obstacles, as the old dirt trail had done, Roman engineers found ways to keep their roads straight. Sometimes they built up a section of road, or cut out a terrace, so that they could keep on a straight line past all but major barriers.

The new roads' surface was made of very large rocks, cut to fit together and provide a smooth, flat face for the roadbed. They were laid on top of a bed of gravel to provide good drainage and a solid base. When these structures were done, they would support not only foot soldiers and light wagons, but the heaviest weapons for war known at the time.

Road Workers. Who built the Heraclean Way? Over the 150 years that this road was built, many different people worked on it. Some were soldiers not needed for war during a temporary peace. Sometimes soldiers on active duty helped build the roads to their own garrisons.

Often the Romans used local workers. These might be paid, or they might be slaves from other parts of the emerging Roman Empire. They might also be "free" men from the area who were "pressed into service," that is, forced to work on the road.

Whoever they were, they did a good job. The road was so well built—and so well maintained over the next six centuries—that you can still see many remains of the road if you visit Spain today.

Rome's Influence on Iberia

Like the Carthaginians before them, the Romans brought a more stable kind of life to Iberia. The trade they established allowed for more local people to move into the new, Roman-built cities. The cities in turn created new markets for food, so other local people became farmers.

The Road of Silver. Increased trade meant increased demand for the rich resources of the mines of Spain. Merchants and traders carried these products out of the mines onto the Heraclean Way, where they could be carried to Rome and the cities of the east. One feeder road leading out of the silver mines brought so much silver along its path that it was called the *Via Argenta*, or the *Road of Silver*.

New Trade. Many products went to coastal seaports as well. These ports became more important as Rome began to want more imported food and supplies than could be carried by land. Rome began to depend so much on the products of Hispania that it forbade Alpine people to grow grapes and olives; Rome wanted to be the only place that Hispania could trade with to get grapes and olives. Rome wanted to be sure of having something valuable to trade for Hispania's goods.

Hispania became more and more important to Rome. Over the centuries, some of Rome's finest writers came from Hispania, including Martial, Lucan, and both Senecas. Two Roman emperors, Hadrian and Trajan, were also born there.

ROMAN INFLUENCE ON GAUL

The Romans were also consolidating their military hold on Gaul. Besides building the Heraclean Way, they built a series of forts, some of which later became the French cities Aix-en-Provence and Narbonne. Even though the mountains above the coastal strip were still beyond Roman control, the coastal plain was firmly in the grip of Rome. The Romans called it *Provincia*, which means "province." From this the area gets its modern name, *Provence*.

Provence was so settled and Romanized that the Roman writer Pliny the Elder said that it was "more like Italy than a province." Cicero agreed, noting, "All Gaul is filled with traders and is full of Roman citizens."

After Julius Caesar had spent some time in Hispania as quaestor (a financial official) and Roman consul, he went on to conquer the interior of Gaul for Rome from 58 to 50 B.C. After that, even more traders and moneylenders moved in along the coast. Colonies for disabled or retired veterans were also established along the pleasant Mediterranean Coast.

To many people, Gaul was a kind of paradise, with minerals, grains, and animals in abundance. The minerals proved disappointing, since they were mined out quickly. But the rest was true, and Gaul provided even more goods for the traders. The Gauls provided new markets as well. They were eager for the luxuries introduced by the Romans, including wine from Hispania.

NEW CHALLENGES TO ROME

The Romans continually faced new challenges in the form of various invaders who threatened their rule. Such outside invaders would one day play a major role in the decline of the Roman Empire. Meanwhile, the Romans dealt with them both militarily (trying to subdue them through force of arms) and politically (trying to persuade them into the Roman Empire as loyal subjects rather than confronting them as outside threats).

Celts and Romans. One group that continued to challenge the Romans was the Celts. The Celts' original home was in southwest Germany. They spread rapidly over Europe in the fifth and sixth centuries B.C., inhabiting parts of what are now the British Isles, France, Spain, Italy, Macedonia (in Yugoslavia), and Asia Minor (where Turkey is). Forms of a Celtic language were until recently spoken in Ireland, Wales, parts of Scotland, Cornwall and the Isle of Man, and in Brittany in northwest France.

Throughout the early Roman period—that is, the second and first centuries B.C.—the Celts held the mountain passes of the Alps. Therefore, Roman traffic between Italy and Iberia had to go by sea or by the coastal land route. Even on the coastal land route, however, the Celts threatened the Ligurian part of the Heraclean Way.

Eventually, the Celts were subdued by Caesar Augustus, the first Roman emperor. Caesar Augustus was the new name taken by Octavian, the nephew of Julius Caesar. After Julius Caesar was assassinated, Octavian and his ally, Marc Antony, fought a civil war against Brutus and Cassius, the assassins of Julius Caesar. Then Octavian fought a second civil war against Antony and Antony's ally, Cleopatra, queen of Egypt. When Octavian triumphed, he became Rome's first emperor and took the name Caesar Augustus.

After Augustus subdued the Celts in the Alps, he appointed a native prince, Cottius, to improve the road over the Mont Genèvre pass. In recognition of his work, the area was named the Cottian Alps.

A Dangerous Road. The road through the mountains was far from easy, however. Even four centuries later, in the fourth century, soldiers feared this route, as described by Ammianus Marcellinus, a soldier himself:

> [The road is] terrible to look on because of the overhanging cliffs on every side ... [It is especially frightening in] the season of spring, when the ice melts; then over precipitous ravines on either side and chasms rendered treacherous through the accumulations of ice, men and animals descending with hesitating steps slide forward ... [and] wagons as well ... [The men] bind together a number of these vehicles with rope and hold

them back from behind with men and oxen and proceed at a snail's pace. But when the road is caked with ice … travelers oftimes are swallowed up.

Roman Milestones. Despite the obstacles, the Romans did gain control of some Alpine passes, as well as of the Heraclean Way. They were proud of controlling Hercules' entire route to the Atlantic, and all along the way they posted *milestones*—stones carved with the number of miles between them and the ocean. These milestones were the ancestors of today's highway markers. We also use the word *milestone* to mean a significant event in the progress of someone's endeavors.

At the same time as they were enlarging their network, the Romans developed another ancestor of a modern artifact—the travel book. Books were regularly produced that told travelers the best routes to take, which dangers to watch out for and where they might find a place to eat or sleep along the route.

ABGADES VSQVE

ADPORTVM	XXIIII	VAEENTIA	XX
HASTA	XVI	SAGTNTO	XVIII
VGIA	XXVII	ADNOVLAS	XXII
ORIPPO	XXIIII	ILDVM	XXII
HISPALIM	IX	INTIBILI	XXIII
CARMONE	XXII	DERTOSA	XXVI
OBVCLA	XX	SVBSALTV	XXRVI
ASTIGI	XV	TARRACONE	XXI
ADARAS	XII	PALFVRIANA	XVI
CORDVBA	XXIII	ANTISTIANA	XVI
ADDECVMO	X	ADFINES	XVI
ADLVCOS	XVIII	ARRAGONE	XX
VCIESE	XVIII	PRAETORIO	XVII
ADNDVLAS	XIII	SITERAS	XV
ADARAS	XIX	AQVISVOCON	XV
ADMORVM	XVIIII	GERVNDA	XII
ADSOLARIA	XVIIII	CILNIANA	X
MARIANA	XX	IVNCARIA	XV
MENTESA	XX	INFIRENEO	XVI
LIBISOSA	XXVIII	RVSCINNE	XXV
PARIETIMIS	XXII	COMBVSTA	VI
SALTIGI	XVI	NARBONE	XXXII
ADPALEN	XXXII	BAETERRAS	XV
ADARAS	XXII	CESSERONE	XII
SAETASI	XXVIII	FORODOMITI	XVIII
SVCRONE	XV	SEXTANTIO	XV

SVMMA MILLIA

Silver itinerary goblets showed all the 106 stops between Gades (Cadiz) and Rome on the Heraclean Way, by the Mont Genèvre route. (From Konrad Miller, *Itineraria Romana*, 1916)

The 1,700-mile Heraclean Way became so popular that artisans made silver mugs shaped like milestones. These showed the route, city by city, along the Heraclean Way.

Roman Travelers

Wealthy Travelers. Travel meant different things to different Romans. For some, it was a chance to show off wealth and status. Hundreds of two-wheeled chariots might be assembled by a single wealthy traveler, who would decorate the chariots with embossed metal plates. Horses, mules, muleteers (mule drivers), and slaves would all be dressed in traveling cloaks, often of bright red. Costly furniture would be packed for use on the road, so that when the procession stopped for the night, the rich owners might make camp with their own beds, tables, and chairs.

Because city streets were overcrowded, riding and driving were forbidden in Rome and most other cities, except at night. So journeys generally started at the city gate. Travelers would be carried to that point on pillow-covered litters (covered cots) by six to eight slaves. Travelers would then transfer to private chariots or coaches. Women travelers often rode in two- or four-wheeled closed carriages, to give them privacy. Servants usually rode in rougher wagons.

On the way, scouts would be sent ahead to learn the condition of the road and to arrange for repairs, if necessary. One very extravagant traveler, the Roman Emperor Caligula, required local people to sweep their roads and spray them with water to keep down the dust. Other travelers simply had to bear the dust and the heat. It may be difficult to think of travel as hot and dusty if you picture riding in a closed car on an asphalt road. But imagine riding down a dirt road, or even a paved one, in an open carriage, with horses hooves' and carriage wheels biting into the road!

At night, wealthy and powerful travelers would stay with friends or would set up their own luxurious camps beside the road. The progress of an emperor often seems to have been a heavy burden for local people. The writer Pliny wrote a description of the Emperor Trajan, praising his modest ways—and contrasting the ways of earlier emperors, who were not so modest!:

Now [with Trajan] there is no disturbance over requisitioning vehicles, no haughtiness in receiving entertainment. The same food suffices for the emperor as for his suite. How different was the journeying of the other emperor [Domitian] in days not long past, if indeed that was a journey, not a devastation, when he carried off the goods of his hosts, when everything right and left was brought to rack and ruin, just as if those very barbarians from whom he was fleeing were falling upon the place.

Modest Travelers. Most people traveled more modestly on the Heraclean Way. A closed four-wheeled coach was sometimes used to transport a whole family. Such vehicles were also used as stagecoaches for individual travelers, who were thus forced to ride side by side with strangers. Drivers and porters of these vehicles were under government supervision.

Other travelers could afford and preferred litters, even on the road. These litters were carried by slaves, or sometimes were slung on poles carried by two mules, one at the front of the litter, one behind. Such travelers were sheltered behind curtains and could sleep, read, or write if they wanted to. As Plutarch describes it, Julius Caesar was one such traveler. Caesar made many trips on the Heraclean Way. Although Plutarch makes no mention of how his slaves bore the journey, Caesar was supposed to have traveled with great speed, since:

> For the most part, Caesar slept in his chariot or in litters, so that he could still be active even though he was resting ... He traveled with such speed that he needed no more than eight days to reach the Rhodanus [The Rhone River] from Rome.

People whose tastes were even simpler might drive their own chariots or ride a horse or mule.

Of course, many travelers went on foot. Instead of making their own camps, they ate and slept at inns along the road. Those who traveled light might sleep under a pine tree, or in the shelter of one of the many tombs that lined the main road.

Couriers and Spies. Riding past the foot travelers and the slow-moving litters were the high-speed couriers on their swift horses. Soon after Caesar Augustus conquered the Heraclean Way, he established an imperial postal service to carry messages between Rome and its conquered territories.

The postal service depended on stations along the early Heraclean Way, where a courier could change horses. At this stage, the service carried only the messages of officials of the Roman Empire. The Roman army also maintained a system of couriers—though some called them spies. The military couriers were called *peregrini*, which

The Romans built this magnificent stone bridge across a river near their colony of Nemausus (modern Nîmes, France); the top part was an aqueduct, carrying water to the townspeople. (From James Henry Breasted, *Ancient Times: A History of The Early World ...,* 1914)

means "wanderers." Private people, if they were rich or powerful enough, also hired riders or runners for their personal business.

Merchants and Traders. Merchants carrying goods along the Heraclean Way had to pay customs duties at the border of each new province. This made the land trip expensive for merchants, leading many of them to prefer the sea route.

Although it was cheaper, the sea route could only be taken from late spring to early autumn. After that, bad weather made the sea too dangerous. So rough wagons hauling heavy cargo also joined the stream of traffic on the Heraclean Way.

THE FALL OF ROME

When the Heraclean Way was the main lifeline of the Roman Empire, it was relatively secure for travelers. But as the empire expanded and the armies spread out to distant borders, it became less protected. Highway robbers, who were often among the conquered people, increased in number. In the third century A.D., for example, a band of over 2,000 people menaced the Heraclean coast road between the cities now called Genoa, in Italy, and Nice, in France.

Christianity. At about the same time, Christians began to travel on the Heraclean Way in order to spread the word about their new religion. Christianity was the religion of those who believed that Jesus was the son of God. It began where Jesus had lived and died, in one of the eastern provinces of the Roman Empire called Palestine.

At first, only a few scattered people believed in this religion. They traveled westward along the roads of the Roman empire, telling others about their ideas. Gradually, the new religion took hold, spreading throughout Europe in all directions.

The Eastward Shift. Meanwhile, the Roman Empire was weakening, unable to keep a strong military hold on its far-flung territories. The center of the empire was shifting from Rome itself to Byzantium, a city in the East. Byzantium was made capital of the Roman Empire by the Emperor Constantine. Later, the city's name was changed to *Constantinople* in his honor. (Today the city in modern Turkey, is called *Istanbul*.)

Constantine made another important change: in the early fourth century, he converted to Christianity and made it a legally practiced religion within the empire.

Christians had developed a practice of making *pilgrimages*, or religious journeys, to the places they considered holy. One such place was Jerusalem, in Palestine, where Jesus had preached. Constantinople became an important stop for pilgrims traveling from Europe to Jerusalem.

Constantinople soon eclipsed Rome itself. By the early fifth century, Rome was very weak. Waves of Germanic peoples began pouring down toward the Heraclean coast, invading the Roman Empire and eventually destroying it. The Roman government itself fled from Rome, leaving it to the invaders.

After the Fall of Rome. When Rome fell, the Heraclean Way could no longer be a single, continuous, protected route. No one power controlled all of its 1,700 miles. The original people of the former Roman territories began a long retreat away from the coast, up to the hills. There they could protect themselves from the Goths and the Vandals, the invading peoples sweeping down from Germany into Gaul and Hispania.

Pilgrims still made their way along the Heraclean Way, but with difficulty. They had to be willing to face great dangers in the form of robbers, invaders, and long stretches of isolated territory without inns, food, or shelter.

Travel for pleasure on the Heraclean Way, obviously, became a thing of the past. Traders, however, continued along the route as they had done for several thousand years. But their trade was at a much lower economic level. No longer did they have the luxurious goods of Roman artisans to barter with, nor the silks and jewels of the east, which other traders had brought into Rome. The collapse of Rome meant that there was much less communication among the different parts of the world, and therefore less trade of different types of goods.

The road itself was left without any kind of maintenance. Indeed, local people often took rock out of the road's paving to use it for buildings of their own. As the road's condition became worse, carts and carriages could not travel upon it. Travelers turned more to walking and riding, developing bridle and footpaths along the cracking and overgrown paved road.

In this time, called the Dark Ages, the Heraclean Way was divided among many different peoples. The Visigoths, a Germanic tribe, controlled the Spanish portion and the Gallic coastal strip up to the Rhône River. The Franks, another Germanic tribe and the ancestors of today's French, held a key section between Marseilles and Nice. East of that was Lombardy, held by the new invaders called the Lombards (whose descendants are the residents of Lombardy, a region of Italy).

The final section of the Heraclean Way was for some time part of the Eastern Roman Empire. But when Rome finally fell, that section of the road was included in the Papal State—a Christian territory that was the ancestor of today's Vatican, the headquarters of the Catholic Church.

The Heraclean Way was no longer a main highway joining united lands. It had little value except as a local road.

The Influence of the Moors

In the eighth century, another people expanded their empire into the land around the Heraclean Way. Strong armies from the Moorish people of North Africa crossed the Mediterranean and entered Iberia (modern Spain). They quickly took control of this land and called it *al-Andalus*. From this word comes the adjective *Andalusian*, which is used to refer to Spanish culture or customs.

Islam and the Moslems. The North African armies were from a people that practiced the religion of Islam. This religion is followed by those who believe that, while Adam, Noah, Abraham, Moses, and Jesus were also great prophets, the last of God's prophets was a man called Muhammad.

This Moslem prophet lived in Mecca, in what is today the country of Saudi Arabia. There he founded Islam early in the seventh century. The Moslems still consider Mecca their holy city. From Mecca, the new religion spread quickly through Arabia, the Middle East, and North Africa, reaching the height of its influence between the ninth and 11th centuries. (The Moslems date 622, when Muhammad was forced to flee Mecca, as their year 0.)

Moslems in France. Both because they were a rival empire and because they were a rival religion, the Moslem Moors met strong resistance when, after conquering most of Spain, they tried to move into France. The Franks were led by a man called Charles Martel, whose nickname was "the Hammer." As Charles' nickname suggests, he was a strong military leader and he stopped the invasion of the Moors in 732.

Meanwhile, Arab pirates had attacked the Gallic mid-section of the Heraclean Way. Some of them even established their own bases along the Gallic coast. Destruction was so widespread that few records remain from this period.

The Moors in Spain. Some of the Moors had recently been nomads, wanderers in the deserts of North Africa. These invaders were astounded by the amazing array of buildings, bridges, and roads that they found in Spain. According to the Arab geographer al-Bakri these accomplishments were "attributed to one of the ancient Kings of al-Andalus whose name was Hercules."

But also among these Moslem peoples were some of high culture, who carried with them the heritage of the great Eastern civilizations of Egypt, Syria, North Africa, as well as that of Greece. While many in Europe had come to forget the Greek culture, the learned Moslems had preserved it.

While the Moslems were in Europe, they converted many Europeans to their religion as well. They paid little attention to the roads of al-Andalus, using them as they found them. What they were interested in was founding a high culture, in which Moslems, Christians, and Jews lived together peaceably. Members of the different religions worked together, intermarried, and even shared

More than 2,000 years after it was founded, Cadiz (Gadir) was still a prominent port. (From G. Braun and F. Hogenberg, *Civitates Orbis Terrarum*, Cologne, 1576)

their houses of worship, since each of their Sabbaths fell on a different day of the week.

While the Moors were in Spain, sea trade declined along the western coast. The old port city of Gades—now called Cadiz—at the end of the Heraclean Way became less important. Some of the highest centers of Moslem culture were found eastward along the old Heraclean Way, notably at the cities that became known as Còrdoba and Seville.

The Expulsion of the Moors.

Although the Moors made many great contributions while they were in Spain, they were never able to establish a stable central government. They were frequently under attack from Christian rulers, who wanted to regain control of the land. Gradually, the Christian nobles were able to expel the Moors.

Ferdinand and Isabella, the monarchs who gave Columbus his chance to explore the Americas, were also the rulers who presided over the final expulsion of the Moors in 1502. They also expelled the

Jews from Spain, sending them into exile in Europe and North Africa.

DECLINE OF THE HERACLEAN WAY

Crusaders Along the Route. The Crusades comprised a series of efforts made by Christian soldiers, nobles, and traders throughout the 11th, 12th and 13th centuries to recapture Palestine from Moslem rule. Palestine had once been part of the Roman Empire, and thus had been under Christian rule when the Roman Empire had made Christianity its official religion. Palestine was also considered holy by the Christians because Jesus had lived and died there.

While some Crusaders were inspired by religious motives, others were more interested in enriching themselves or in expanding trade with the East. Only the First Crusade had any success at all, and the Crusaders were never successful in recapturing and holding the Eastern lands.

However, the Crusades did have quite an impact on the Heraclean Way. The Italian ports of Pisa and Genoa and the French port of Marseilles saw increased activity in trade due to the Crusaders coming southward to these cities on their way to Palestine. The Crusades also generated an increase in trade with the East through those ports.

Modern travelers to Rome have often deserted the coast road for the inland route past Pisa, with its famous leaning tower. (By A. H. Hallam Murray, *Sketches on the Old Road Through France to Florence,* 1904)

City-states. At this time, Genoa, Pisa, and Marseilles were city-states, independent cities rather than part of a larger nation. They

grew stronger as a result of the increased trade. But since their power came from their sea trading, it had little effect on the coast road.

The Condition of the Road. Some parts of the road were rough, but usable. Other parts were barely usable through lack of repair. Even where the road was usable, bandits were a constant threat.

This situation continued from the eighth century and for many centuries thereafter, when travelers on the Egnatian Way would often avoid the rocky coast altogether, and travel by boat.

Rival Nations. The road was not the only problem. It was also difficult to cross between all the small kingdoms through whose territories the road passed. Each kingdom had its own customs duties and tolls. In some places, the borders zigzagged across the roads. Then merchants might have to pay several tolls for the same stretch of road—a practice that certainly discouraged trade and travel!

Squabbles between warring states also made trouble for travelers. For example, some states harassed merchants who were traveling to or from rival states. There were reports of other states

With the Heraclean Way in disrepair, travelers sometimes hired fishermen like these at Menton to sail them around the mountainous part of the route. (*Peoples of the World,* 19th century)

actually destroying bridges to make travel more difficult. (Of course, a kingdom might want to destroy a bridge to make it more difficult for invaders to pass, as well.)

The road itself had become little more than an eight-foot-wide dirt track. It was most difficult in the rocky section above the French city of Nice. This section was known as the Corniche. The French lady-in-waiting Madame de Genlis wrote in 1780 that:

> In many places the Corniche is so narrow that it is difficult for anyone to pass … at all the really dangerous places we dismounted and made the passersby hold our hands.

Some people would hire a boat from local fishermen to sail around the most rocky regions, preferring to expose themselves to the dangers of the open sea rather than to those of the road.

NAPOLEON AND THE HERACLEAN WAY

At the turn of the 19th century, the Heraclean Way attracted the attention of Napoleon Bonaparte, who was also interested in the Alpine passes. He wanted to build an empire as powerful as Rome had been, and he understood that in order to do so, he needed roads.

This Italian woman set up her loom by the side of the Heraclean Way, skirting the Mediterranean in Tuscany, once land of the Etruscans. (By A. H. Hallam Murray, *Sketches on the Old Road Through France to Florence*, 1904)

Napoleon and the French Revolution. Napoleon was a leader who came to power in France out of the confusion following the French Revolution. In 1789, the French began a struggle that overthrew their hereditary system of monarchy and leadership by the rich, and founded a republic of the people based on the principles of liberty, equality, and fraternity. That is, every man was supposed to be equal.

Naturally, this revolution provoked both civil war in France and war between France and many other European nations whose monarchs and aristocrats did not want a new, more democratic regime to survive. Napoleon served as an officer in the French Army, winning attention for his brilliant military abilities.

Many different regimes fought for power in France during and after the Revolution, constantly reforming the republic into other varieties of government. In 1799, Napoleon was set up as "first consul," or dictator of France. He made peace with the countries who had been fighting France as a result of the French Revolution and in 1802 he became first consul for life.

The Napoleonic Wars. In 1803, however, Britain declared war on France. Napoleon had himself crowned emperor of France in 1804 and went on to fight the British while conquering other lands of Europe, starting with Italy. Through the so-called Napoleonic Wars, the whole map of Europe was rearranged.

As part of his military empire-building, Napoleon embarked on a roadbuilding campaign, which included modernizing the eastern part of the old Heraclean Way. Napoleon built the famous road that still exists, the Grande Corniche, on the modern border between France and Italy, running over mountains 1,400 feet above sea level.

During the same period, the prince of Monaco built another road, lower down, along the coast, known as the Lower Corniche, or Route de Littoral (Coastal Route). Both roads were important factors in increasing travel and trade between France and Italy.

However, Napoleon's main route south was through the Alps, and thus he improved several Alpine passes, which again served the purpose of connecting France to Italy. The Napoleonic Wars brought turmoil to Europe for decades. Napoleon's final defeat occurred at the battle of Waterloo in 1815. His roads, however, continued as a monument to his impact.

In the early 19th century, travelers began once again to rediscover the French Riviera. This discovery began almost accidentally. In 1834, British politician Lord Brougham was forced to stay in the small fishing village of Cannes due to an outbreak of cholera in Nice. He found the place delightful. Travelers soon discovered what the Romans had known long ago, that the Riviera was as beautiful as it was healthy.

The Changing Map of Europe. In the mid-1800s, the city-state of Nice chose to unite with France. Monaco, however, remained an independent kingdom, and today is one of the smallest nations in the world.

Italy, on the other hand, was able to unite all the separate Italian city-states. The border between France and Italy was then set, so that the eastern half of the Heraclean Way was split in two.

Vacations for the Rich. In the early 20th century, both the French and the Italian Rivieras became popular with the rich and

In modern times, Antibes and other Riviera towns have become health and pleasure resorts, as in Roman Times. (By A. H. Hallam Murray, *Sketches on the Old Road Through France to Florence*, 1904)

privileged. The many beautiful bays and beaches along the Heraclean Way made the Rivieras very attractive. At the time, the Corniches were probably the best roads in the world, for they were funded by the revenues raised from tourists—and the tourists were generally wealthy.

Monaco pioneered a road improvement method, the use of tar on roads. This practice quickly became widespread elsewhere.

The 50-mile-an-hour speed record for automobiles was first set at Nice in 1901. By that time, according to the historian, Hermann Schreiber, the Grande Corniche saw about 500 automobiles, the same number of horse-drawn carriages, perhaps 200 motorcycles, and a few hundred rough carts daily. Imagine what this scene must have been like at a time when very few people except the rich could afford a car or carriage.

As the south of France and Italy became more popular with the wealthy, it was featured as a setting more often in novels. The beautiful landscape seemed an ideal setting for romance, with the gambling casinos of Monaco adding a touch of adventure that continues to attract people today.

Spain and the Heraclean Way

The western half of the Heraclean Way was witness to a different history in the 19th and 20th centuries. When the Christians had moved down to conquer and expel the Moors in the 15th century, the center of government had shifted from the south, where the Moors had been strong, to the north, where the Christians had more power. The Spanish capital of Madrid, as well as the Portuguese capital of Lisbon, were at the centers of their countries. Thus the Heraclean Way was pulled farther north.

Southern Spain had lost its political power, but still possessed an air of romance due to its colorful history and culture. Many tourists were drawn to southern Spain and passed along the old Heraclean Way to reach their destination.

The Heraclean Way Today

Today the old Heraclean Way is a route for tourists, often traveling in their private automobiles. They can ride along the Spanish coast, the Provence coast, and around the Rhône delta, or follow the

The road on the cliff below Cannes is in direct line from the Heraclean Way, which skirted the Mediterranean in Roman times. (By A. H. Hallam Murray, *Sketches on the Old Road Through France to Florence*, 1904)

spectacularly beautiful Riviera through France and Italy to Rome, the ancient hub of the world.

Indeed, so many tourists pass this way that a new route—the Middle Corniche—was built out of Nice just before World War II. There visitors follow the ancient way of Hercules, on the cliff-face above the palace of Monaco and below the old hill route of the Caesars.

Suggestions for Further Reading

Braudel, Fernand. *The Mediterranean and the Mediterranean World in the Age of Philip II*, two volumes (New York: Harper & Row, 1972 and 1972), translated from the French by Siân Reynolds.

Charlesworth, Martin Percival. *Trade-Routes and Commerce of the Roman Empire* (London: Cambridge University Press, 1924).

Chevallier, Raymond. *Roman Roads* (Berkeley and Los Angeles: University of California Press, 1976), translated from the French by N.H. Field.

Devoluy, Pierre and Pierre Borel. *The French Riviera* (London: The Medici Society Limited, 1924).

East, W. Gordon. *An Historical Geography of Europe*, third edition (London: Methuen, 1948).

Leighton, Albert C. *Transport and Communication in Early Medieval Europe, A.D. 500–1100* (Newton Abbot; David Charles, 1972).

Murray, A.H. Hallam, accompanied by Henry W. Nevinson and Montgomery Carmichael. *Sketches on the Old Road Through France to Florence* (New York: E.P. Dutton, 1927).

Rostovtzeff, M. *The Social and Economic History of the Roman Empire*, two volumes, second edition, revised by P.M. Fraser (Oxford: Clarendon Press, 1957).

Schreiber, Hermann. *The History of Roads: From Amber Route to Motorway* (London: Barrie and Rockliff, 1961), translated from the German by Steward Thomson.

Semple, Ellen Churchill. *The Geography of the Mediterranean Region: Its Relation to Ancient History* (New York: Holt, 1931).

Sitwell, N.H.H *Roman Roads of Europe* (New York: St. Martin's, 1981).

Skeel, Caroline A.J. *Travel in the First Century After Christ: With Special Reference to Asia Minor* (Cambridge: University Press, 1901).

Trend, J.B., *The Civilization of Spain* (London: Oxford University Press, 1944).

Von Hagen, Victor Wolfgang. *The Roads That Led to Rome* (Cleveland: World, 1967).

5

THE ORIENT ROUTE

THE GLAMOUR OF THE ORIENT EXPRESS

The Orient Express—the luxury train that traveled across Europe into the very heart of the East—has captured the imagination of romance and mystery writers for generations. Diplomats, spies, lords and ladies, bankers, and explorers took this train from Paris, France, to Constantinople, Turkey, passing through Vienna, Budapest, and Bucharest. In any one of the elegant railway cars, you might meet an Austrian aristocrat, a British big-game hunter, a deposed noble from Eastern Europe, or a French countess. The reality of this train may even have been as romantic as the writers portrayed it!

Traveling between east and west has often been very difficult. Ever since the days of the Greeks and Romans, different empires and political powers have fought for control of the European territory that lies between western Europe and Asia Minor (where Turkey is located). In addition, the territory between east and west is often mountainous, rocky, or otherwise difficult to cross.

However, there was one route that crossed Europe and Asia to connect east to west. This was the route followed by the Orient Express railway itself—the famous Orient Route.

THE SCOPE OF THE ORIENT ROUTE

The Orient Route was set by early traders, built by the Romans, and used by medieval Christian pilgrims and Crusaders. For centuries, one portion of it or another was used by various peoples for various purposes. But until modern times, it was not a continuous main road, joining all the various countries it passed through. Rather, it

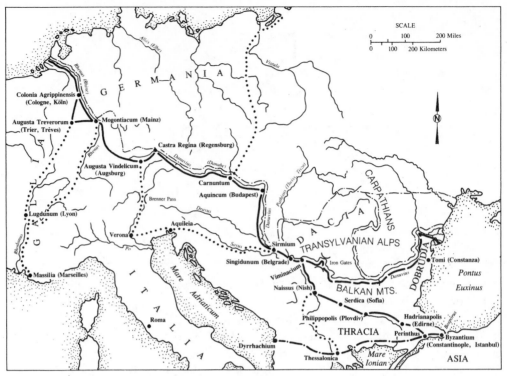

The Orient Route in Roman Times

——————— Main Road   —— —— — River Route   —— —— — Roman Frontier
—— —— — Egnatian Way   · · · · · · · · Connecting Routes

was a series of makeshift paths, some of them better maintained than others, enabling travelers to pass across sections of difficult and sometimes dangerous terrain.

The Danger of Invaders. The eastern part of the Orient Route—the section between the upper Danube River and Istanbul, Turkey—has always been exposed to invaders. Over the centuries, this territory has passed back and forth among various invaders, empires, and military powers.

There were always ways to cross this territory. But because of the constant threat of attack in this area, the Orient Route was not often used as a major highway. Sometimes the major highways ran across the route; other times the route was simply neglected. Only once before the Orient Express—during the Crusades of the Middle Ages—did the Orient Route become a really major highway.

Dangers of the Danube.

Dangers of the Danube. Many sections of the Orient Route run alongside the Danube. Thus travelers could sail on the Danube River for part of the eastward trek—but there were often good reasons to go by land, instead.

The Danube River could be hazardous. Near the city of Orsov, for example, is a narrow gorge called the Iron Gates. The name helps you to imagine how difficult it must have been to pass between the narrow, rocky walls of the gorge in a little boat! To make matters even harder, the gorge was full of great, frothing rapids that might overturn any craft traveling by water.

To be safe at the Iron Gates, travelers would have to unload their goods and *portage*—carry or drag the goods and the boat—to the next usable part of the river. Portaging made travel more difficult and more expensive.

Thus the Danube had heavy traffic in some parts, but little traffic in others. Also, the Danube flows eastward, toward the Black Sea, whereas travelers were more likely to travel southeast to the city of Istanbul, gateway to Asia Minor. Thus for both safety and con-

The swift currents of the Danube's Iron Gates have throughout history caused difficulties to boats headed upstream. (Yugoslav National Tourist Office)

venience, travelers were more likely to choose the land route over the waterway, even though in many places the two wind side by side.

Geography of the Orient Route. The Orient Route starts at Istanbul, in Turkey, on the Bosporus Strait between Europe and Asia. From there, it passes west across Thrace (a region that includes parts of Greece, Bulgaria, and Turkey) until it reaches the Danube River, near Belgrade, Yugoslavia. Then the route passes through Budapest, Hungary; Bratislava, Czechoslovakia; and finally to Vienna, the capital of Austria.

Of course, the nations of Europe were very different when people first began using the Orient Route! And this part of Europe probably changed more often than most, as invaders and empires continued to fight over its rich territories.

EARLY HISTORY

New Skills. In early times, the area past the southern end of the Orient Route held the most advanced peoples of Europe. Residents of this part of the Middle East developed new skills: stoneworking, farming, metalworking, and herding.

To appreciate what this meant, you have to picture what life must have been like for the early peoples of Earth, before they knew how to grow food, how to tame animals, or how to make things out of metal and stone. People of that time ate only what they could gather themselves, with their bare hands. The new skills discovered in this part of the world helped change all that by giving people the ability to grow more food than they needed, and thus have surplus food to trade with.

These new skills spread quickly from Asia Minor across the Bosporus Strait into Thrace. They stopped at the Iron Gates, which acted as something of a natural barrier. If it was difficult to cross them in later times, imagine how difficult it would have been before people knew how to make things out of metal or stone!

The peoples of the Danube River developed these new skills and created their culture. They were known as Indo-Europeans, and were the ancestors of the Greeks, Germans, Celts (ancestors of the modern Irish), Gauls (ancestors of the modern French), and many other peoples. These groups would eventually come to rule Europe and much of western Asia.

The First Traders. From about 3000 B.C. to about 1000 B.C., this region was fairly stable. Few people came into it or left it. The culture grew, based mainly on what happened inside the region.

There was some communication with the outside, however. From 2000 B.C. to 1000 B.C., wandering traders traveled through the region in four-wheeled wagons and two-wheeled chariots! They had adopted these new-fangled means of travel from the East.

Then, in about 700 B.C., wandering nomads called the Scythians invaded from the Steppes—the wide, grassy, prairie-like lands that stretch across the southern part of the Soviet Union.

The nomads had not settled down to grow food—partly because the steppes were not the type of land that was easy to cultivate. Instead, they wandered from place to place, gathering food as they went.

The Scythians did know how to tame and ride horses. This meant that they could fight on horseback, which gave them a great advantage. They would ride along the coast of the Black Sea toward the fertile plains of Hungary, bringing great disruption to the region.

After the Scythians came, trade and travel were in turmoil. They did not revive on the Orient Route until Greek times.

THE GREEKS

The Greeks developed a culture that flourished over 2,000 years ago in the country around the Aegean Sea. Greek scientists and philosophers invented many of the concepts that Western culture lives by today. Greek artists created a style of art that still influences Western art and people's ideas about what is beautiful. In many ways, Greek culture was the beginning of the overall culture of Western Europe.

The Greeks moved into the Black Sea region at about the same time as the Scythians. The Greeks entered the region not on horseback, but by boats and on foot. They were traders along the Danube River.

At first the Greeks traded only up to the Iron Gates. Later they went farther, at least as far as Belgrade, Yugoslavia.

The Greeks themselves were probably unsure how far they had gone. Some early Greeks actually thought that Western Europe was an island, cut off from the mainland of Russia by a great channel formed by the Danube and the Rhine River. Of course, we know these two rivers don't actually meet—but they do come within 50 miles of each other in the Black Forest of Germany.

The Orient Route's First Trading Post. It was the Greeks who founded the southern end of the Orient Route. In the seventh century B.C., they set up a trading post they called Byzantion on the European side of the Bosporus Strait. Then they traveled between Byzantion and Belgrade, trading.

However, the Orient Route was still small and unimportant. It would not become a major highway until the Roman era.

ROMAN TIMES

The Romans were a people who gradually conquered most of Europe and of nearby Asia. The Roman Empire shaped much of the history of Europe, even up to the present day. Countries that were formerly occupied by the Romans tend to speak languages that are derived from Latin, such as French, Spanish, Portuguese, Rumanian, and Italian. They also tend to be countries where the Catholic religion is dominant, stemming from the time when the Catholic version of Christianity was the official religion of the Roman Empire.

Because they had conquered so many nations, the Romans were able to build and maintain roads uniting many different parts of the world. Although the roads were originally built to transport armies from one part of the empire to another, they were also used to make trade between all parts of the empire easier.

Of course, it took the Romans many hundreds of years to extend their military power to its height. They did little on the Orient Route in their early days; their focus was the west. Therefore, as late as the second century B.C., the only eastern territories that Rome held were on the coast of the Adriatic Sea and the Egnatian Way, from Illyria (Albania) to Byzantion, which they eventually renamed Byzantium (see Chapter 2).

Rome Expands. By the first century A.D., however, the Roman lands were being attacked from the east. The Roman legions attacked in turn. They fought the peoples of Eastern Europe along the Danube.

These people were fierce fighters. The strongest of them were the Dacians, who lived in what is now Rumania and eastern Hungary. The first Roman legions to cross the Danube—using a wooden bridge

Trajan's column in Rome celebrates not only great battles but also more homely events like the crossing of the Danube from a fortified city. (Forum Traiani, Rome)

they had built for the purpose—were massacred by the hard- fighting Dacians.

Finally, the famous Roman emperor and general, Trajan, conquered the region. To hold it, he built up the forts along the Danube and built a road along the frontier, to make it easier for soldiers to go where they were needed. This road became the basis of the Orient Route.

Rome Builds Roads. It wasn't easy building a road along the Danube. There are many gorges there, with little level ground to create a highway. Trajan's engineers had to have the roadworkers actually carve a road out of sheer rock. The road had to be wide enough for a wagon to pass, so that soldiers' supplies could be transported as well as the soldiers.

How do you suppose the roadworkers of these early times solved such a difficult construction problem? Sometimes they built the road out over the river on wooden balconies that were fitted into holes made in the rock. Sometimes they simply carved out the rock itself. For many years, you could still see the Roman channel, until a modern dam and canal project finally covered it with water.

The Romans were quite proud of their construction. They set up plaques and monuments to praise themselves, both for being good engineers, and for triumphing over the Dacians. This road meant that soldiers could travel quickly to any point on either the Danube or the Rhine Rivers, along with wagons full of heavy supplies or weapons.

Roman Cities. Trajan and later Roman rulers also founded, rebuilt, or renamed many of the main cities along the Orient Route. One such city was then called Serdica, settled 2,000 years before and named for the local Serdi tribe. Today it is called Sofia, and is the capital of the country of Bulgaria.

Sofia/Serdica was a fortress that the Romans used to guard the Orient Route. So were the cities of Singidunum (today, Belgrade) and Aquincum (modern Budapest). They formed the main line of the Orient Route.

Trajan's Bridges. Trajan also built bridges across the Danube. Some were pontoon bridges—bridges that floated, resting on barrels, but sturdy enough for soldiers and wagons to cross. Other bridges were more permanent, built on stone piers for extra strength.

One of Trajan's most impressive bridges was the one he built over the quarter-mile-wide Iron Gates. Decades later, the Roman Emperor Hadrian destroyed the bridge, so that Rome's enemies could not cross over it and fight more easily with Roman soldiers. But even the bridge's ruins were impressive. As the Roman writer Cassius wrote many years later, "[The] piers are [still] standing ... they seem to have been erected for the sole purpose of demonstrating that there is nothing that human ingenuity cannot accomplish."

The Road Grows. As you can see, the Orient Route was mainly a military route to the Romans. The first rough tracks were made by roadbuilders traveling with the Roman army.

Later these builders would be joined in their work by the soldiers, in order to construct the long-lasting roads that Rome needed to hold the frontier. In other parts of the Roman Empire, these improved military roads were used by traders and pleasure travelers as well. But pleasure travelers and even traders used only part of the route.

Rome Turns East. After the Roman empire had stood at the height of its powers for two centuries, it focused its attention almost entirely on the east. Many of its emperors were born in the east, some along the Orient Route itself. Many spent large parts of their careers defending the frontier marked by this highway.

This shift to the east was marked by the founding of a second Roman capital. In the early fourth century, the still-small city of Byzantium was rebuilt and renamed once again. This time it was called Constantinople, in honor of the Roman Emperor Constantine.

Constantine was famous for another great change—he made Christianity a legal religion in the Roman Empire. Christianity is the religion of those who follow the teachings of Jesus and consider him the son of God.

By the end of the fourth century Christianity was less than 400 years old, but it had grown from a few followers of Jesus in the territory of Palestine to an organization with the strength of Rome behind it. However, most of the peoples in Europe were not yet Christian. They still followed their own, older religions.

At about the same time that Byzantium was renamed, the Bosporus Strait was becoming the main crossing point between Asia and Europe. From now on, Constantinople would be the gateway between the two continents.

THE FALL OF ROME

After several centuries of power, Rome began to decline. New waves of nomadic peoples were coming down from the Eurasian steppes, challenging Roman rule. Soon they were pouring through the once-secure Roman frontier line—marked by the Orient Route.

In the fourth century, Rome tried to bring its Germanic neighbors into the empire, trading with them and settling them along the Roman frontier.

But in the fifth century, a new people invaded—the Huns. These people came from the plains of what is today the country of Mongolia. They were powerful warriors and broke through the frontier. The core of the Roman Empire was no longer protected.

The Invaders and the Orient Route. For the Orient Route, these invasions were a disaster. The invaders destroyed the main cities on the route. Some of the cities were not rebuilt again until modern times.

Worse than that, many people were frightened of the invaders and tried to run away from them. As the invaders pushed toward the Hungarian plain, they pushed the Germanic population in front of them, leading to great confusion as people left their homes, families, and villages.

Because the Hungarian plain was so easy to cross, it was the target of many different invading peoples over several centuries. Some of these peoples included the Goths (A Germanic people who lived for a time in France); the Huns, Avars, and Magyars (ancestors of the modern Hungarians); and the Slavs (ancestors of those in such heavily Slavic countries as Russia, the Ukraine, Yugoslavia, and Czechoslovakia).

Each invasion left the Orient Route territory poorer and with fewer people than before. Large sections of land were no longer farmed as the farmers ran away to safety. The nomads used these lands as pasture for the herds of cattle and horses that they took with them on their wanderings.

THE MIDDLE AGES

Early in the Middle Ages, the Orient Route fell into disuse. Trade and traffic from the northern seas no longer reached the Black Sea via the Rhine and the Danube. It came instead by the Russian river routes opened up by the Slavs and later by the Swedish Vikings. These new routes went much farther to the east and led to the development of different countries and different peoples.

The picture only began to change in the 10th century. Unlike the other nomadic invaders, who retreated back to the Eurasian steppes, the Magyars stayed in the Hungarian plain. They became part of the European peoples. At this time, many Europeans were Christians, and the Magyars also converted to Christianity.

CHRISTIANITY ON THE ORIENT ROUTE

Pilgrimages. The 10th century also saw the rise of Christian *pilgrimages*, or religious journeys. Christians would travel to places in the world that they considered holy, including the city of Jerusalem, where Jesus had preached.

Christians had been making pilgrimages to their Holy Land since the fourth century. That was when the Roman Emperor Constantine converted to Christianity and made it a legal religion in the Roman Empire. As part of his new devotion, he rebuilt Jerusalem and other religious sites in Palestine.

Pilgrimages happened infrequently in this early period, but by the 10th century the pilgrimage movement began to take hold. For a variety of reasons, people wanted to travel to Jerusalem in larger numbers than ever before. Many would-be pilgrims lived in northern Europe, so for them the Orient Route was the best way to go to Asia Minor.

Islam: Another Religion on the Route. This overland route through Constantinople to Palestine took Christian pilgrims into the territory of people of a different religion—Islam. Islam was founded in the seventh century by Muhammad, who is supposed to have received revelations from God which he recorded in a book called the *Koran*. This book is to the followers of Islam—called Moslems—what the Bible is to Christians and Jews.

Islam recognizes Adam, Noah, Abraham, Moses, and Jesus as prophets of God, but says that Muhammad was the last of God's great prophets. Muhammad founded this religion in Mecca, which is the Moslem's holy city, to which they make pilgrimages. Mecca is located in what is today the country of Saudi Arabia. However, Islam quickly spread throughout the Middle East and Northern Africa from the eighth through the 11th centuries.

Although the Christians passing through Constantinople were of a different religion than the Moslems, the two groups had managed to live side by side, peacefully, for centuries. The Christian pilgrims brought money and business into the Near East, and respected the religious differences of their hosts. Then, in the 11th century, the situation suddenly changed.

THE CRUSADES

In the 11th century, a new group arrived in the Near East, the Seljuk Turks. This group had newly converted to Islam and they held it above all other religions. They decided that they did not want Christians passing through their land, and they cut off the pilgrimage routes to Jerusalem. They also attacked the Christians who were living in the region. At that time, Constantinople was still a Christian city, so there was a large number of Christians in the surrounding area.

The *Pope*, head of the Catholic Church and at that time leader of all the Christians in Western Europe, decided that the Christians should fight back and even escalate the fight. In 1095, he urged Christians to go to war and to take the Middle Eastern land that they considered holy away from the Moslems. This began a series of wars known as the *Crusades*.

The Crusaders had a variety of motives. Some of them were truly religious. Others were fighters looking to make their fortune, or nobles looking for land and loot. Many of the Italian cities who sent Crusaders were influenced by merchants who wanted to expand trade with the east.

The Peoples' Crusade was formed to regain the Holy Land, but the Peasant Army killed thousands upon thousands of Jews and Eastern Christians on the way there. (1525, authors' archives)

The People's Crusade. One part of the first series of crusades was called the People's Crusade. It began in the spring of 1096. Tens of thousands of Christian pilgrims gathered together in France and Germany. They were inspired both by the Pope and by wandering preachers like Peter the Hermit and Walter the Penniless. As you can tell from the names, these preachers were humble men, far removed from the power of the Pope. You can see also that this part of the First Crusade attracted many poor people.

The People's Crusaders formed small bands and began working their way east. Most of these pilgrims were rough and wild. Perhaps they had been eager to go on the Crusade because they were bandits fleeing the law. Or perhaps they had not been able to get work, or to make their fortunes, and so they were desperate and willing to try anything.

Some of these early Crusaders were inspired by sincere motives, but some of the People's Crusaders did not wait to fight the Turks! Instead, many began attacking those they considered "God's enemies" even while they were still in Europe. As they headed east, they murdered those with whom they did not agree—and also, perhaps, those from whom they could steal.

The German groups were especially murderous. They massacred Jews in the German cities all along the Rhine River, and in Bohemia (a region of modern Czechoslovakia). The Jews were members of a religion even older than Christianity. They believed in the same God that the Christians did, but did not believe that Jesus was the son of God. In this period, they were often under attack by Christians. Again, those who attacked them had both religious motives (the Jews were not Christians) and economic ones (the Jews could be robbed by those who attacked them).

Eventually, all the separate groups of People's Crusaders met on the upper Danube River. By this time, they had a well earned reputation as bandits. This army of 100,000 people headed toward the East, looting and stealing from people along the way.

In fact, the People's Crusaders had little money with which to make their journey. They had gotten some money from contributors who believed in their mission. But there was little food to be had in Bohemia, Hungary, and the Balkan Mountains (now part of Bulgaria). Even the small local population did not have much to eat, so you can imagine how difficult it must have been when another 100,000 people suddenly arrived.

The Crusaders were angry at the high prices charged for the little food there was. Some of them even fought Christians along the way, in order to take more food. They attacked the citizens of Belgrade, capital of today's Yugoslavia and then under the control of Hungary. The angry king of Hungary made a full-scale counterattack and killed thousands of Crusaders.

Many Crusaders fell by the wayside, too. They were in a state of near starvation and exhaustion from walking for over four months through the rugged hill country of the Balkans.

Even so, when the Crusaders finally reached the plain before Constantinople, they were a frightening sight. Anna Comnena, daughter of the emperor whose capital was Constantinople, saw the Crusaders as "a countless people ... more numerous than the sand of the sea ..."

At that time, Constantinople was the capital of the Byzantine Empire. This had once been a part of the Roman Empire, which had been Christian. Later, the Christian Church split into two parts—the Catholic part, which followed the leadership of the Pope in Rome, and the Eastern Orthodox part, which followed the lead of the Byzantine emperor, based in Constantinople. Although Moslems now lived in the Byzantine Empire, there were also many Christians living there, too.

The Crusaders were supposed to be allied with the Christian Byzantines. Instead, they attacked many of their communities. Because these Christians were not part of the Catholic Church, the Crusaders did not consider them "real" Christians.

Then the People's Crusade moved across the Bosporus Strait into Asia Minor. There they kept on attacking all local Christians. They treated all Asians as *heretics*, people who did not follow the Christian religion. And they were ready to kill or attack all heretics.

Finally, the People's Crusaders met the Moslem Turks, who cut them to pieces in battle. Those who were not killed were enslaved. Few if any ever reached their goal of Jerusalem.

Professional Knights. Though the People's Crusaders were ill-prepared and ill-fated, the Christian knights who followed them were not. Some of them came from Flanders (a region in modern-day Belgium and the Netherlands) and Lorraine in France, taking the Orient Route. They met up with the other knights at Constantinople. From there, they crossed Asia Minor and defeated the Seljuk Turks. Afterward, they carved out a series of Christian states in the Near East.

The Second Crusade. However, the Christians continued to lose land to the Turks, so they embarked on a Second Crusade. Knights on this Crusade also traveled on the Orient Route. They gathered at various points in northern Europe and eventually met on the upper Danube River. From there they traveled slowly, on foot, going only 10 to 20 miles a day. It took them three months to go from the lower Rhine River to Constantinople.

The army of the Second Crusade was large and varied. It included the royal leaders, King Louis VII of France and his wife, Eleanor of Aquitaine (a play was written about Eleanor's later years, called *The Lion in Winter*). The army included many nobles and professional knights. But it also had outlaws who were allowed to choose between going on the Crusade and being hanged on the gallows.

The army made quite a show. A description is recorded in a book called the *Gestes de Louis VII (The Deeds of King Louis VII)*:

> Anyone seeing these cohorts with their helmets and bucklets shining in the sun, with their banners streaming in the breeze, would have been certain that they were about to triumph over all the enemies of the cross and reduce to submission all the countries of the Orient.

There were also many women in the army. The Byzantine historian Nicetas describes them like this:

> ... there were in the army women dressed as men, mounted on horses and armed with lance and battle axe. They kept a martial mien [appearance], bold as Amazons [legendary warrior women]. At the head of these was one [Queen Eleanor] in particular, richly dressed, that went by the name of the "lady of the golden boot." The elegance of her bearing and the freedom of her movement recalled the celebrated leader of the Amazons.

Despite its good show, the Second Crusade ended in dismal failure. There were several other crusades over the next two centuries, but eventually the Christians had to give up the idea of capturing the lands of the Middle East.

LOCAL TRADING ON THE ORIENT ROUTE

Even without having to fight the Turks, it was hard to cross Asia Minor. People began to use sea routes to get to Jerusalem, bypassing the Orient Route.

Some supplies did travel on the Orient Route. But even the cities on the upper Danube did not get their supplies this way. Instead,

With trade on the Orient Route disrupted, cities like Vienna were often served by merchants from Italy or Germany, like these from Berlin. (From *Toggenburger Bibel*, mid-16th century, Kupferstichkabinett und Sammlung der Zeichnungen, Berlin)

their supplies came over the Alps along the Brenner Pass Amber Route (see Chapter 1).

The Orient Route and the Danube River once again saw mainly local trading. Partly, this was because the route was hard to travel, but it was also because the places on the route did not make trade or travel easy for foreigners. Many cities charged duties, which were expensive. Some of them demanded the right to handle all transport, which meant that traders had to hire transportation from them, at their prices. Sometimes cities even confiscated goods. Under these conditions, the Orient Route could not become a through highway.

The Ottoman Empire

There was also a good deal of fighting on the Orient Route at this time. In the late 11th century, there were more invaders from the steppes moving onto the Hungarian plain. The Pechenegs (also known as Patzinaks), Cumans, and Bulgars (ancestors of today's Bulgarians) pushed a wedge between Hungary and the Byzantine Empire, and split the Orient Route.

Then, in the 13th century, Hungary was attacked again by the Mongols (ancestors of today's Mongolians). This further increased the difficulties of traveling on the Orient Route.

Meanwhile, the Byzantine Empire was continuing to shrink. As the religion of Islam had spread in the Middle East, the Christian empire of Byzantium had become smaller and weaker.

These 13th-century Mongols were simply part of a long line of invaders flooding onto the Hungarian plain. (New York Public Library)

Constantinople. At the same time, the empire's capital city of Constantinople was becoming a mere shell of its former self. Constantinople had been seized by Crusaders who saw their Catholic Church as more holy than the Byzantine Eastern Orthodox Church. The city was then controlled by various Italian city-states from the outside.

Therefore, by the late 14th century, it was relatively easy for the Ottoman Turks to push from Asia Minor into Europe. They took piece after piece of the old Byzantine Empire, converting it from Christian into Moslem territory, until finally, in 1453, they took Constantinople.

The Ottoman Turks made this city the main base for their *Ottoman Empire.* From Constantinople, they easily overcame other people on the lower Orient Route. The Ottoman Turks now faced

Christian Europe, and the two groups would battle over the Orient Route for decades to come.

The Ottomans Expand. The city of Belgrade was the Ottomans' first target. Even before they had taken Constantinople, they had already taken the city of Sofia (capital of today's Bulgaria). Belgrade was the next logical city to attack—and they finally captured it in 1521.

The capture of Belgrade left the city of Vienna open to siege. Since the late 13th century, another empire, ruled by the *Hapsburgs,* had used Vienna as its base. For the next two centuries, the Hapsburgs and the Ottomans fought each other.

Twice the Austrians took back Belgrade, but always the Turks won it back again. The Turks tried to take Vienna, but the rest of Europe sent assistance and Vienna remained unconquered.

The Lower Orient Route. The Ottomans were trying to expand westward, while still maintaining control of the lower Orient Route. The people who lived in this area were still mainly Christians.

The Ottomans also ruled over the Gypsies, a nomadic people who had been pushed out of the area that is now Iran as they fled from the conquering Turks.

Thus there were many religious and ethnic groups in this region. They made an uneasy peace with one another, but they rarely mixed. Byzantine Greeks were of the Greek Orthodox branch of Eastern Orthodox Christianity. They became the bankers, merchants, and officials of the new order. Bulgarians took camel or horse trains along the Orient Route, bringing food from Hungary and Rumania for Constantinople. Gypsies were on the route as wandering tinkers [repair people], musicians, and horse traders.

The Difficulties of Travel. During the 15th and 16th centuries, there was some travel on the Orient Route. During periods of peace, the Turks even made some trade agreements with their Christian neighbors.

Nevertheless, travel was still very dangerous, both by land and by river. The ships that traveled on the Danube were heavily armed and ready for attack. Land conditions were even worse. Armed robbers awaited travelers at every weak point, especially at shaky wooden bridges or at *fords* (places where a river is shallow enough to be crossed on foot).

For many centuries, the Turks seemed unbeatable. During this time, the European Christians were weakened by wars among themselves. The Catholic Church was challenged by the rise of *Protestantism*, a new version of Christianity that did not recognize the authority of the pope or of the Catholic Church's organization. Instead, Protestantism stressed the individual's direct relationship to God, without the need for priests or the elaborate church structure. At this time fierce religious wars flared up between Catholics and Protestants.

Early in the 18th century, the Austrians were able to push the Turks back to Belgrade. The Turks continued to hold Belgrade for another 150 years, but their domination of the Orient Route had already begun to decline.

With Austria's new expansion, more traffic began to sail on the Danube River. In addition, the roads were improved. Without fear of the Turks, the Austrians could get rid of the old wooden bridges that could be taken apart quickly when an enemy came. Now they wanted permanent, sturdy bridges for peaceful uses.

The Danube was good for downstream travel. But upstream travel—travel against the current—was very difficult, dangerous, and expensive. It took eight boatmen, 40 horses, and 30 drives to bring just one load of grain upstream from Pest (part of the Hungarian city of Budapest) to Vienna—and the trip took a whole month.

The river also had cataracts, gorges full of rushing rapids that made travel dangerous. River barges could not sail over cataracts. They had to be unloaded, made lighter, and carried over land until the barrier had been passed. This hauling and carrying was heavy work. Often it was done by convicts sentenced to hard labor, since no one could be found to do it voluntarily.

Steamboats and Sandbars. The coming of the steamboat in the 1830s made a huge difference to traffic on the Danube. Suddenly traffic upstream was much faster and much cheaper.

The cataracts of the middle Danube were still a problem, however, especially at the infamous Iron Gates. Some parts of the river still made it necessary for travelers to go by land.

People found many ingenious ways around the difficulties. Sometimes they were able to blast deeper channels, so that the boats would be able to sail on deep water.

In other places, sandbars were a problem. A sandbar is a huge pile of sand that has built up on the river bottom. Sometimes river boats would get stuck in sandbars, especially if the sandbar lurked just below the surface of the water. Sailors on the Danube followed an old Turkish custom. They put a rake behind their ship, trailing through the water, so that it would help to flatten the sand that the ship might have stirred up. This helped to prevent sandbars and make river travel safe for all.

THE ORIENT EXPRESS

While the Danube water route developed, the Orient Route on land was not used very much. But as soon as railroads appeared in Europe, all that changed.

At first, the railroads of the Orient Route were mostly local lines. But a Belgian financier and train-lover, Georges Nagelmackers, had a dream. He wanted to build a railroad that would cross the many cultures and countries of Europe.

Europe in the Late 19th Century. At the time of Nagelmackers' dream, European countries and their boundaries were very different

On its way southeast across Europe to Istanbul, the Orient Express route would later follow the left bank of this gorge 200 miles south of Belgrade. (Yugoslav National Tourist Office)

from what they are today. Many different empires controlled huge territories, having power over countries and peoples that today are independent. These empires were constantly trying to expand, taking land or power away from other empires. Although there were several small wars, the world seemed to be at peace—until 1914, when these empires would fight each other bitterly after a small incident set off a war that seemed to involve the entire world—World War I.

Nagelmackers' Early Dream. In the period before the war, however, such a catastrophe was unimaginable. Nagelmackers could easily envision a railroad that would link the countries of Europe to one another and to Asia.

Even under peacetime conditions, Nagelmackers' work was hard enough. His early projects were all failures. He wanted to build a train from Paris to Berlin, but in 1870 the Franco-Prussian War between France and Germany put an end to the plan.

Then Nagelmackers wanted to build a railroad from Belgium's post of Ostend to the Italian city of Brindisi, the last stop on the old Appian Way (see Chapter 2). But the French blasted a tunnel through the Mont Cenis Pass in the western Alps and built a shorter, faster route to Brindisi. Once again, Nagelmackers' plan was a failure.

The plush cars of the Orient Express train featured in innumerable tales. (Authors' archives)

The determined train-lover did not give up. He began to put together a luxury railroad line. At that time, the United States' Pullman Company had developed the *Pullman Car*, a luxury railroad car that made train travel attractive to the rich. Nagelmackers used these cars as a model for trains that made short runs between Paris and the cities of Western Europe. This was the beginning of what was to become the glamorous railway line, the Orient Express.

Royal Help for the Orient Express. From the start, Nagelmackers had royal support—perhaps because King Leopold II of Belgium owed him money! He needed friends like that, to make contracts with eight different railroad lines in half a dozen countries, and a shipping line besides.

Many Borders, Many Problems. As we have seen, Nagelmackers had a lot of political issues to consider as he put his luxury railroad together. There were national rivalries such as the rivalry between France and Germany, either of whom might take any sort of action to make things difficult for the other country. There was also the dangerous situation in the Balkans, the multinational center of what today is Yugoslavia, where many different peoples and different empires quarreled and negotiated, trying to gain control of the region.

In addition, there had been recent wars between Turkey and Russia. Finally, there were peoples who were trying to break free of the empires that controlled them and were getting ready to wage wars of independence.

Because of such problems, Nagelmackers' railroad never followed one single line. Its route varied with political conditions. Some parts of the line were traveled by train. For others, passengers had to go by ship or ferry. Passengers on the first journey of the Orient Express went from Paris, through Germany, Austria, Hungary, Bulgaria, and on to Constantinople.

Red Carpet for the Orient Express. The idea of a train that could cross Europe and go into the Orient excited people's imaginations. Reporters began to call the line "the Orient Express." (An "express" is a train that goes somewhere very quickly.)

Passengers on the Orient Express's first trip in October of 1883 received the red carpet treatment all the way. Royalty greeted them at every stop, often with dinners and entertainments. Not all of these greetings were pleasant. In Rumania, passengers had to walk in the rain on a muddy road, just to reach the king's castle!

On the other hand, passengers enjoyed the Gypsy band that played and danced for the passengers on a 70-mile part of the trip through Rumania. Most of the passengers stayed with the train on the trip back. Most seem to have agreed with French writer Edmond About, who called it "eleven wonderful days of a unique and historic journey."

Growth of the Orient Express.

Growth of the Orient Express. On its first trip, the Orient Express was right on schedule. Usually it stayed pretty well on schedule even on later trips—but the weak link was the part of the journey where passengers had to sail across the Black Sea. Since sea conditions could not be predicted, neither could the schedule.

Nagelmackers wanted to solve this problem by having his own trains take passengers all the way to Constantinople. The Turks finally agreed to this plan. Even so, trains could not make the trip all the way along the route, for the Balkan region under Turkish rule was still very poor and isolated. It was too difficult to build train tracks through this area.

Nagelmackers' solution was to build a road link between Turkish railroads in the south and his Orient Express in the north. This link was a "flying coach," like an old stagecoach, drawn by horses. Passengers much preferred their comfortable Pullman cars to the bumpy ride of a coach along a rocky or a muddy road! Even on good roads with fast horses, these coaches could go only 10 to 12 miles an hour. On the rutted, muddy tracks of the Balkans, three to four miles an hour was more usual, with the baggage wagons going even more slowly than that.

In addition to discomfort, the passengers faced danger. These flying coaches, full of wealthy riders, were prime targets for robbers. Their windows had to be made especially small, for protection against brigands' bullets. The railroad company had to pay for armed guards.

Finally, in 1889 the rail connection was completed. For the first time, passengers were able to ride directly across Europe, from Paris to Constantinople, without leaving their railway cars.

Success of the Orient Express. Passengers on the Orient Express included royalty, government officials, and wealthy business travelers. But the train also attracted tourists, who wanted to see the striking scenery of the Alps, the Danube, the Balkans, and

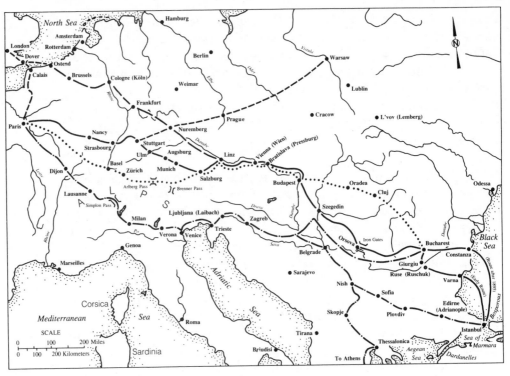

The Orient Express Routes in the 1920s

——————— Orient Express

—·—·— Simplon Orient Express

········ Arlberg Orient Express

— — — Ostend Orient Express

-------- Main Connecting Routes

romantic Constantinople. The Turks called their capital city "Stamboul," so some people took to calling the famous train "the Stamboul Express."

Imagine the mix of people you might meet on the Orient Express. Perhaps an Indian prince, visiting Paris for the first time, or a British explorer, who planned to connect with an expedition in Constantinople. French writer Paul Morand wrote of the wealthy Americans, "their portmanteaux [briefcases] stuffed with gold coins for bribes in exchange for some new oil concession," as well as Turkish sultans, Polish counts, and mysterious financiers on some errand to fix yet another loan for the Czar of Russia; and diplomats traveling to and from one of the many conferences somewhere in Europe to discuss the status quo and to postpone some war.

Unfortunately, the diplomats could not postpone "some war" indefinitely. There were too many empires in Europe, each wanting more power than the others. What should have been a relatively minor incident in the Balkans—the assassination of an Austrian noble—set one empire against another. There were so many alliances and counter-alliances that soon every nation in Europe was involved in the First World War.

Even after World War I had cut off service on the Orient Express, the line managed to survive, and eventually to expand. After World War I, the map of Europe was redrawn. The great European empires were carved up into many new independent states. The defeated nation of Germany lost much of its power in a treaty that gave lands and money to its old rival, France. Many observers predicted that Germany would not submit to this for long. Another war seemed inevitable and only a matter of time.

Even so, the Orient Express expanded its services and added new lines. By one route or another, passengers could leave Paris for Constantinople (renamed *Istanbul* in 1930) any day of the week. The period after World War I saw great days for the Orient Express.

The Decline of the Orient Express. But eventually this romantic train line ran into hard times. Germany had never really wanted to have the Orient Express cross its territory.

Out of the anger and frustration that the defeated Germans felt after World War I, the Nazi Party was able to come to power, promising to conquer the rest of the world and make Germany the most powerful nation. When the Nazis came to power, they sabotaged the Orient Express trains whenever they could.

In 1938, the Nazis occupied Austria. Then they cut off both the original Orient Express line and a new line that had been added. A third line ran until 1940. Then the Nazi leader Adolph Hitler convinced his Italian ally Mussolini to stop traffic on the route.

Hitler and Mussolini went on to start wars in Europe and Africa and, with their Japanese ally, in Asia. The Second World War ended with their defeat. But once again, the map of Europe had been redrawn, with new borders and new political regimes taking hold.

After World War II, the Orient Express tried to reopen its old routes. But political problems made that hard to do. There were disputes between Yugoslavia and Greece, between Turkey and Bulgaria, and between several Eastern European countries and the Soviet Union.

These trains had for the first time made the Orient Route a true international highway. Now they faced competition from automobiles and airplanes. In Western Europe, speedy highways took more passengers away from the trains. In Eastern Europe, good roads were far less common. But there travelers often flew over borders to avoid the endless checks of visas and papers that they had to go through every time a train entered a new country.

The Orient Express trains still ran to the East. But gradually they lost their luxury. The last trains did not even have a restaurant car. Passengers had to buy food at local stations—if they could find a way to get local money.

The Orient Express Today

Although regular Orient Express trains no longer cross Europe, there are still some special tourist trains that make the trip. Train-lovers can still follow the old Orient Route, along the Danube, past the magnificent gorges of the Iron Gates, through the striking scenery of the Balkans, to the Turkish city of Istanbul. These riders can still taste the romance and the glamour of the old Orient Express.

Suggestions for Further Reading

Chevallier, Raymond. *Roman Roads* (Berkeley and Los Angeles: University of California Press, 1976), translated by N.H. Field.

Clark, J.G.D. *Prehistoric Europe: The Economic Basis* (London: Methuen, 1974; reprint of 1952 edition).

Cookridge, E.H. *Orient Express: The Life and Times of the World's Most Famous Train* (New York: Random House, 1978).

East, W. Gordon. *An Historical Geography of Europe*, third edition (London: Methuen, 1948), part of the Dutton Advanced Geographies series.

Heichelheim, Fritz M. *An Ancient Economic History: From the Paleolithic Age to the Migrations of the Germanic, Slavic, and Arabic Nations*, in three volumes (Leyden: A. W. Sijthoff, vols. 1 and 2, 1968; vol. 3, 1970), translated into English by Joyce Stevens.

Kendall, Alan. *Medieval Pilgrims* (New York: Putnam, 1970), part of the Putnam Documentary History Series.

Lengyel, Emil. *The Danube* (New York: Random House, 1939).

Lessner, Erwin, with Ann M. Lingg Lessner. *The Danube: The Dramatic History of the Great River and the People Touched by Its Flow* (Garden City, New York: Doubleday, 1961).

Obolensky, Dimitri. *The Byzantine Commonwealth: Eastern Europe 500–1453* (New York: Praeger, 1971).

Piggott, Stuart. *Ancient Europe: From the Beginnings of Agriculture to Classical Antiquity* (Chicago: Aldine, 1965).

Tihany, Leslie C. *A History of Middle Europe: From the Earliest Times to the Age of the World Wars* (New Brunswick, New Jersey: Rutgers University Press, 1976).

Von Hagen, Victor W. *The Roads That Led to Rome* (Cleveland and New York: World, 1967).

Wechsberg, Joseph, and the Editors of Newsweek Books. *The Danube: 2,000 Years of History, Myth, and Legend* (New York: Newsweek Books, 1979).

INDEX

Thrace (region of southeast
  Europe) 42, 110
Tiber River 10, 33, 35, 81
Tin 6, 81-82
Tolls—*See Customs & Tariffs*
Tools 1, 3, 5-6, 8
Tourism—*See Travel*
Tours—*See Travel*
Trade and Trade Fairs
  on Amber Routes 20-23
  on Appian Way 41
  on Great North Road 64, 67,
    68, 69
  Greek wares *35*
  on Heraclean Way 82-83,
    88-89, 94, 96
  on Orient Route 111-112,
    121-122, 124-125
Trajan (Marcus Ulpius Trajanus)
  (Roman emperor) 89, 92,
  113-114
Trajan's Column *113*
Travel and Tourism *27*
  on Amber Routes 3, 12-13,
    27-31
  on Appian Way 46, 56
  on Egnatian Way 46
  on French Riviera 103-104
  on Great North Road 64, 69,
    75
  Guides 18-19
  on Heraclean Way 82-83,
    91-93, 103-105
  on Italian Riviera 103-104

Orient Express and 129-131
  on Orient Route 124-125
  Roman Empire and 46, 91-93
Tristram, W. Outram 72
Trojan War 34
Troy (city) 34-35
Turkey 128
Turks—*See also Ottoman Empire*
  Crusades and 53-55, 119-121
  Egnatian Way and 55-56
  Orient Route and 117
Turnpikes—*See Roads &
  Highways*

U

Union of Soviet Socialist
  Republics—*See Russia*
Utensils 6
Utica (city) 81

V

Vandals (ancient people) 13, 95
Venice (city) 21, 25
Venus (Greek godess) 34
Via Appia—See Appian Way
Via Argenta—See Road of Silver
Viaducts 38
Via Egnatia—See Egnatian Way
Via Herculea—See Heraclean Way
Vienna (city) 124
Vikings 66, 116
Villers, Alexander von 29
Virgil (Publius Vergilius Maro) 34

Visigoths (ancient people) 52, 96
Vistula Route *2*, 7-8, 13, 21, 30
Vlachs (ancient people) 52

W

Wagons—*See Carts*
Wallachs—*See Vlachs*
Walter the Penniless 119
Waterloo, Battle of (1815) 102
Weapons 6
Weaving *101*
West Germany Federal Republic
  of, Germany
Wheat 15
William the Conqueror (William
  I) (England) 67
Winchester (English market
  town) 67
Wine and Spirits 89
Women
  Crusades and 121
  Pilgrimages and 17
Wool—*See Textiles*
World War I (1914-18) 57, 127,
  131
World War II (1939-45) 57, 105,
  131

Z

Zinc 6